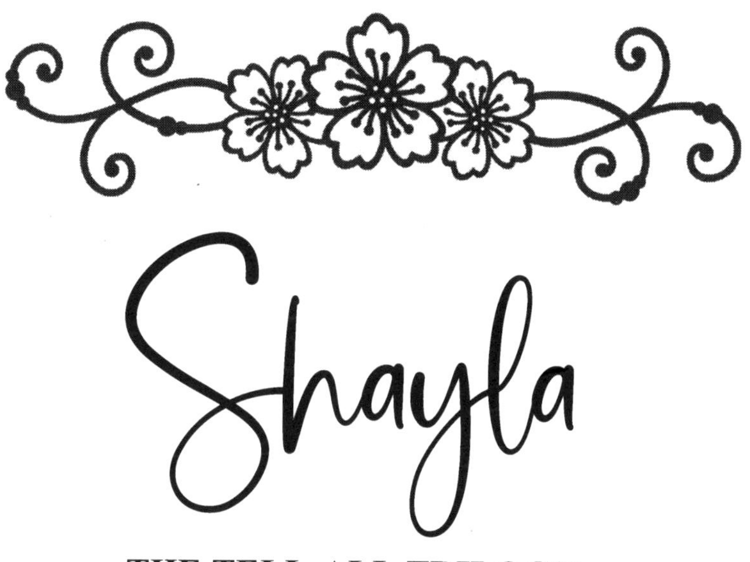

THE TELL-ALL TRILOGY

Regina LaFrance

Shayla

ISBN 978-1506-911-48-9 PBK
ISBN 978-1506-911-49-6 EBK

February 2024

Published and Distributed by
First Edition Design Publishing, Inc.
P.O. Box 17646, Sarasota, FL 34276-3217
www.firsteditiondesignpublishing.com

Published in conjunction with LaFrance Media Group

www.lafrancemedia.com

Disclosure

Note from the Author: I have tried to recreate events, locales and conversations from my memories of them. In order to maintain their anonymity in some instances, I have changed the names of individuals and places. I may have changed some identifying characteristics and details such as physical properties, occupations and places of residence.

This book contains sexual content.

This book

is dedicated to the victims of abuse.

I am further dedicating this book, and making it my mission, to serve as a voice and much-needed light that must be shed on the considerably tragic abuse epidemic of our young and helpless souls.

This story is for you, by one who used to be you.

A special Dedication also to
Lorraine Carlin...
a beloved friend to the end.

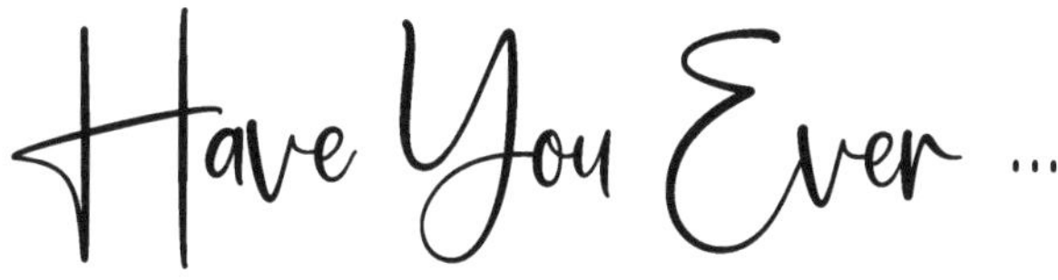

Been repeatedly traumatized?

Hid a dark secret that ate you alive?

Cried yourself to sleep incessantly?

Wished you were not alive?

Tried to hurt yourself?

Blamed yourself for being raped or molested?

Hid yourself from the world because you were too ashamed?

Lived a double life to hide your haunted past?

Read on and discover long-held darkest secrets of a little girl... how this one victim of unfathomable abuse was able to overcome her pain and suffering. Follow her brave journey from trauma to emotional freedom. It all starts here.

Acknowledgements

Were it not for the boundless loving support I have received from my dear and cherished husband, Dan LaFrance, this book would have been a challenge to complete. And for that my Darling, I thank you from the bottom of my heart for being a constant force in my constellation of hope, and for cheering me forward in my vision for telling my story. You are my "rock," my most rigorous critic, my greatest fan, and an ongoing flame to my torch. For *all* of you, Love, I am forever grateful.

I would like to further thank my mentor, my friend and my perpetual anchor, Tany Soussana, who has become my greatest cheerleader and ally, only second to my husband, and a valuable source of inspiration throughout this important journey I have dared to endeavor for bringing my book to life.

Thank you also to my long-lost parents. Gone but never forgotten. They did their best by me in the only way they knew how. For all they have given me, especially during my tender "ladybug" years, *when life was still pristine,* I will always cherish their memory.

To all my friends who never judged me throughout this process of coming forward with my truth, thank you.

And to those who I have hurt at a volatile time while trying to find my way... when I didn't know how to open my heart, my trust, and to love them. To Stephanie Joy and Steven Paul, this means you and I am sorry.

CONTENTS

Introduction

The truth is stranger than fiction that sometimes follows our precious young home.

Shayla is author Regina LaFrance's public outcry. *A calling and a movement.* Inspired by real events, this incredible story could have been prevented—if only her parents would have listened. Her intention for writing this very personal book is to raise awareness with parents to be observant of "signs" at home from their beloved young who depend on their protection.

In this semi-autobiographical bombshell, LaFrance holds nothing back as she reveals the traumatic events of her youth—at a time of innocence when she was too young to speak up, feared for shame, and was reminded to "do her duty" and be a "good girl" by the adults in her life, including her threatening predator, *a pedophile priest,* otherwise recognized as a hero in her religiously devout community.

Shayla is LaFrance's story in more ways than one. It is up to the reader to draw their own conclusions. Novelized to where only the names have been changed, *Shayla* is a shattering account that takes on the persona of LaFrance as a child—when her nightmare started to unfold and escalate to unfathomable enormity forced upon her. Merciless and unyielding, the sacrilege at the hands of her padre marked only the beginning of her brutal deflowering.

LaFrance has come a long way since her native homeland. A place she called home until tragedy struck. She now speaks to the realities of child sexual exploitation, as she has directly and irrevocably succumbed to these heinous acts when her chastity was taken away too soon—*forever shattered and left with only deep-rooted wounds and trauma from her youth.*

Her journey from that dark period has become a lifelong mission at finding emotional freedom; as she would continue to run away from her haunted past. Until it caught up with her future.

> *"From an early age I was a victim of sexual abuse and all I could do was try to hide from the world in shame. I thought the more I would run away from my nightmare, the more I would stop seeing it in my own reflection. My truth. I was just so ashamed of what had happened to me. It left me feeling emotionally crippled and ruined my life. The past ate into my future, raging through me, as if I was being devoured alive. I couldn't function. It seemed like the only thing I could do was to keep my secret to myself in all these years. No one could ever know. I hoped for so long that my past would just fade away into an empty vacuum, like it had never happened. That's all I really wanted... to never look back. To just keep looking ahead and moving forward. I just couldn't risk what people would think of me if they knew.*
>
> *"Now looking back, I don't know what possessed me to believe the world would blame me for being sexually attacked. Alas, a long-held belief that has stayed with me since my childhood. I just thought no one would take my side, or believe me, and I would be persecuted for my predator's actions."*

The writing of this book symbolizes a cathartic release for LaFrance, having come full circle—since the grievous time of these tragic events. In her effort to provide an outlook on hope toward healing and emotional freedom, *Shayla* is about ultimately turning the page on tragedy and moving forward.

For the survivors who have been molested and suffered from abuse, LaFrance is passionate in her perseverance and resolution of this issue. *"It takes strength, courage and belief in one's power to overcome and become greater than our darkness."*

Now enter the world of *Shayla* where letting go to be free from pain, shame and suffering has a chance.

May the pages within speak to your heart.

To all the people who have fallen victim to abuse as children and never had a voice to speak up...
I hear you.
I feel you.
And I am at one with you.
Because I am You.

REGINA LA FRANCE

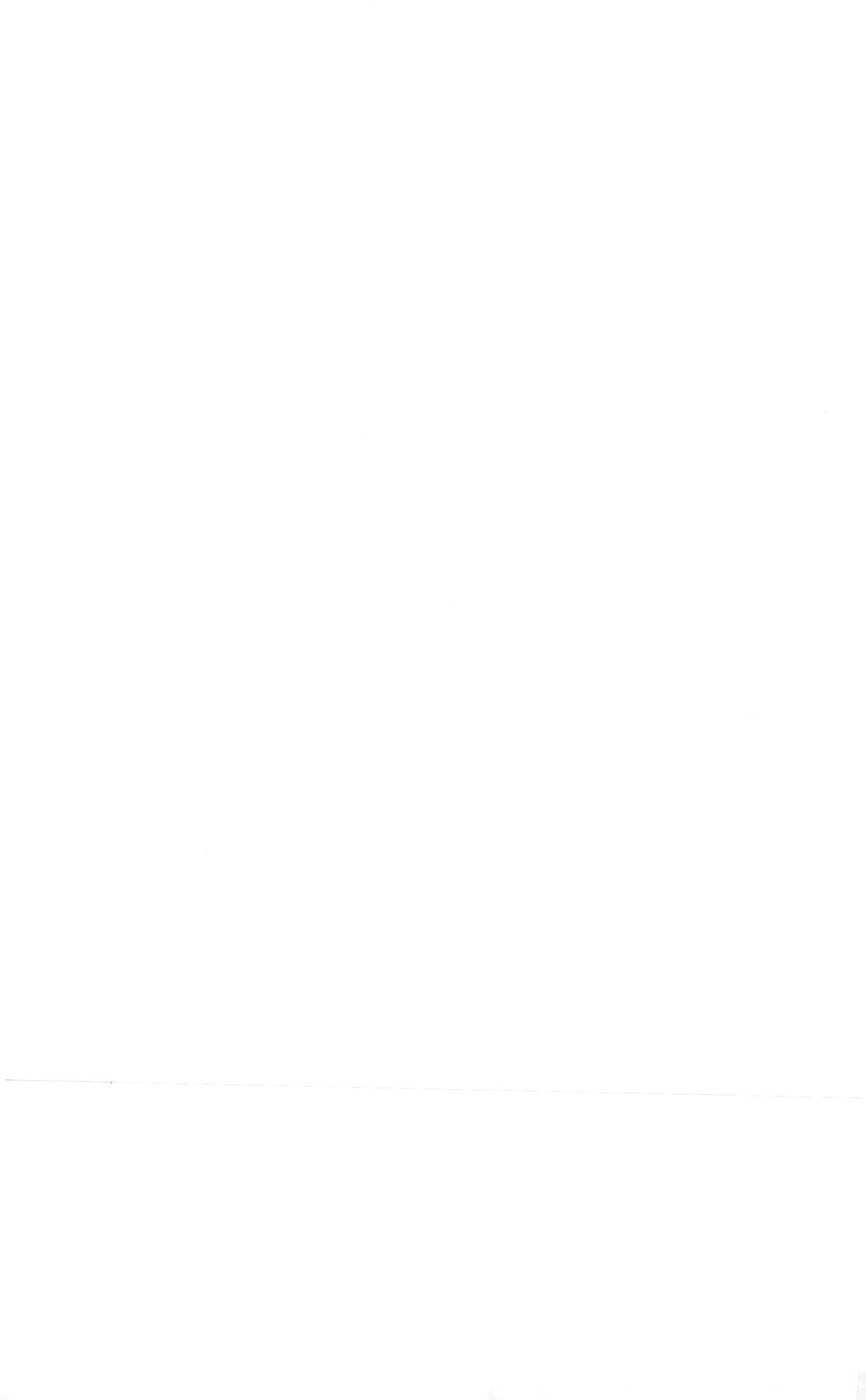

CHAPTER 1

Buried Innocence

Fifty years in the past.

As if the rainy night could have predicted its own fate, the village cemetery felt particularly eerie in the faint shadows of the darkness that blanketed its landscape. The moon gave way to two disproportionate silhouettes emerging against its luminescence. The only brightness in the planned moment of the hour, revealing a somewhat tall, overpowering man, the local priest, wearing his church best. He was accompanied by a young ten-year-old girl, known as Shayla. She was carrying a mysterious small wooden box.

Only moments ago, she had sat in the back seat of his car, thinking he was taking her home. She was gravely mistaken. Instead, he drove to the community cemetery next to his church. A morbid twist was about to ensue with the village hero. In his late forties, his thick protuberant eyebrows brushed an air of camouflage to his balding scalp. With big jutting ears, he bared a familiar resemblance to the classic comedian and actor, Dom DeLuise. Though the priest was horridly furthest from anything bringing levity on this grave night—nor all the other nights that had led to it.

He commanded Shayla to step out of the car and follow him into the cemetery.

The tension of the rainstorm intensified as the sound of thunder seemed to echo the angered heavens looming above the rain-drenched silhouettes in the dead of night. It would not be long as one more dead of the hour was about to join those already laid to rest in the somber landscape. A newest soul would soon become immersed into the grounds, with cause for unforeseen mourning not far behind.

Earlier that evening, Shayla had started to feel severe pains in her lower back area, following the incredible and painful incident she could not understand better at her young age. All she knew was she hurt badly and had curled into a ball outside in the garden of the priest's home where he lived with his mother. How she had gotten to this place, in all its dreadful ramifications, was beyond a bad dream—but a real-life nightmare for the fledgling Shayla.

When she looked up from her embryonic state, fraught and petrified, still suffering in pain, she saw her offender. The priest was standing over her tiny form that appeared reduced as huddled before him. He pointed to get in his car.

A newest soul would soon become immersed into the grounds, with cause for unforeseen mourning not far behind.

As Shayla struggled to get up, trying to follow as instructed, the priest's mother quickly stopped her before getting into the car, handing her a small wooden box with a removable lid and handle wedged on top within the craftwork. The box was no more the size of a shoe box. It was empty and would remain so, until later that night. The young girl would soon discover the purpose for this untimely mysterious box, which held no contents inside. *Yet.*

The priest's hero persona was about to show a brutally divergent side on this frightful night. For little Shayla, furthest from his village recognition, this man symbolized only one wretched identity, that of a monster.

Against the gleam of the moon, he appeared no less. His true self exposed among the buried souls in their stead, no doubt roused by their presence. The girl knew all too well the evil he was capable of, and had committed against her youthful innocence.

Shayla had become the priest's new fallen victim.

With long wavy chestnut hair, she stood rather tall for ten. Once glowing from an earlier innocence of not long ago, she had possessed the light and joy characteristic of a girl her age. Now all but a faded spark forever extinguished by the priest, and only one year following Shayla's first communion.

No one in her inner circle, from family to the villagers, would ever surmise the priest's abhorrent wrongdoing inflicted upon the hapless girl. His *latest* among a string of young female victims in an ongoing pattern, where locals were none the wiser. Until it was too late. Yet, even then, the truth remained shrouded and no one ever really knew all the unpriestly transgressions laid upon their very own. *The young. The innocent. And the unaware.*

Among the flock, Shayla had been violently molested by the unassuming, famous village priest.

If only this night in the cemetery was merely a bad dream she could wake up from.

But the loud sound of thunder served as a further reminder that all was happening in real-time. Alas, the nightmare Shayla had endured at the merciless hands of her predator, the priest, who had brought them to this very moment in the cemetery.

The grounds were surrounded by a tall brick wall with a metal gate to the right of the church. The gate had spindles and it was unlocked on this aberration of a night. No child was ever seen entering the cemetery without an adult for the purpose of bringing fresh flowers to the family graves. They were not allowed alone. Though on this untimely night, things would be quite different. For Shayla, still a child herself, in some sardonic twist of fate, she was accompanied by the most immoral of adults. The priest. His own village worshippers would never suspect or ever know.

The eerie night had incited Shayla's memory, as she recalled the times when she would ask her mother about the tiny graves in the cemetery, as they never had fresh flowers on them.

"Mother, why don't the tiny graves have flowers? Can we plant some?"

"No," answered Shayla's mother. "There hasn't been a baby's death in many years."

"So Mother, there are no dead babies in those graves?"

"Maybe from many years ago, but not that I can remember," said the mother.

Once such a conversation would take place with the small Shayla, she became incredibly quiet as she tried to process her mother's words.

"Do not overthink these things. You are too young to worry or think about adult-only conversations."

Trying to understand the baby graves, Shayla had further prompted, "But Mother, when our neighbor died, you told me it was because he was old and tired. And that's when they die."

"Oh, dear girl, listen up. Sometimes babies get sick too. Any person can get sick and die. Old or young. Just go on and go play. Stop trying to figure out everything."

Perhaps predestined given the night's events, Shayla's concept of "play" by any youthful standard was about to be forever shattered. Her mother could never have imagined what would follow their intimate chats, not too much later and practically fresh off the last one.

Her daughter's inquisitions about death would ultimately bear significant consequence—of the most sadistic nature. Certainly nothing the mother, nor little Shayla, could have prepared for. As an untimely death, too close to home, would eventually shadow their precarious dialogue.

Still inquisitive on one previous occasion, "Mother, why do babies die?"

"Sometimes babies die because God needs an angel."

Fast forward to the cold, rainy and dreadful night in the cemetery, God was about to receive a new angel.

The priest was on a ghastly mission in the cemetery, one of malevolent intent, execrable of every human impulse. He was about to break the very foundation on which his long esteemed local stature was built.

Leading the young Shayla through the graveyard, premeditated and unflinching against the rain, he prepared to do what most had never done since the landscape's beginnings.

However, a stark contrast to burying a cherished loved one, and without ceremony, the burial at stake on this gloomy-destined and misty night was to bury a deed so horrifying, not even the worst of nightmares could have prepared for the atrocity that was about to happen. *A cover-up of the previous atrocious act under the priest's watch and of his own doing.*

The thunderstorm continued to get louder as the priest ushered Shayla toward the area where young infants were buried, next to the gravedigger's shed. To its right, there was a row higher up of exceedingly small graves, designed for babies.

Legend had it that inside this shed, the gravedigger kept far more than just his shovel. Skulls and bones had been found when graves were being dug up for new coffins. The shed had become a curiosity at best, almost a game, among the local children when on the grounds with their adults. They would try to peak at the remains stored in the shed.

Despite being told that if they ever went inside, old souls would pull them in and keep them there, day and night.

The priest had navigated Shayla to the gravedigger's forbidden shed, commanding she go inside.

"Get the shovel," he urged. "Go on!"

She looked at her transgressor, unsure of his next actions, like all the times before that would ultimately lead them to this place. What would soon follow in the graveyard, she could only guess. Though she fought those thoughts with all her young and violated might.

Despite her worst intuitions, the terrified Shayla hesitantly entered the shed. Still shaking from the brutality of her predator. Now also wet and tired. She dared not challenge his overpowering and reprehensible nature.

Nervously fumbling her way forward, inside the pitch darkness of the shed, she tried to find the gravedigger's shovel.

The little girl's shaking was getting worse. Rummaging through the unfamiliar space, her tiny hands tried to feel across the small area until she felt a sturdy handle. She glided her hand down its shaft until she felt the sharp angular metal base of the shovel. Relieved, she grabbed it.

She looked at her transgressor, unsure of his next actions, like all the times before that would ultimately lead them to this place.

Shayla turned around to make a quick exit from the frightful shed, she heard a sudden crackling sound. Like a break. She had just stepped onto some bones among the debris of remains left in the shed. Rushing through the door, she saw the priest standing just outside, puffing nonchalantly on a cigarette. Completely devoid of guilt from his vicious acts against the girl.

He led her to an open spot among the baby graves. "Start digging a hole," the priest commanded Shayla as he presided from a distance, where he continued to smoke his cigarette—like any other tool bringing him pleasure that he thought nothing more about.

The helpless girl had become to him similar to the butt of his next smoke. A tiny instrument of pleasure, fallen prey to the worst adult act forced upon a child. The priest was callously amused and emboldened by her fear of him. How could she not be afraid of him? Considering all she had endured under the subterfuge of his priestly cloak, shrouding his menacing ways.

Shayla's young and small world had been turned upside down, erupted beyond return, as she faced this very real demon in her life. Furthest from his priestly image, so adored by the locals, he had become an abominable villain bent on performing the evilest of sins on a juvenile.

Part of his throng of devout followers, Shayla's parents looked up to him. The priest could do no wrong in their eyes.

Yet, the unthinkable was about to happen on the unfathomable night. The unrelenting rain became a mere reflection of the priest's abysmal actions. Terror in Shayla's eyes, she started digging a hole. The priest motioned for her to drop the rain-soaked wooden box she had been carrying into the dug hole, leaving it uncovered.

In a vertigo spiraling fog, as if waking from a nasty lucid dream, echoes of her loud scream from sudden excruciating pain reverberated across the graveyard. She next heard the priest's voice as he handed her a towel.

"Go ahead and clean yourself. Then get dressed and cover the hole."

Suddenly the night's events came into clearer focus for the lost and bewildered Shayla. The unimaginable for a little girl was done. Her aborted fetus had just dropped into the box. Weak and in shock from the realization of what had happened, she tried to grasp her bearings as she felt the pain from the strange rush of waste that had left her body.

No longer in a fog state, the priest pointed a flashlight into the hole she had just stepped away from, and with his foot, kicked the lid to the box into the hole. She looked down between her feet, gazing at the hole, where it was only moments before she had gone into shock—a daze of confusion, mixed with utter and unimaginable shame. She was sobbing and still in pain. In a trance-like state, following the beam from the priest's flashlight, Shayla picked up the gravedigger's shovel and started to fill the freshly dug hole in the earth with loose dirt from a small pile nearby her feet. She shuddered in denial, not able to bring herself to recalling the details of what had just transpired on the rainy night, amid the newly covered hole. *Now a grave site in the cemetery—only moments ago, virgin grounds, as was young Shayla.*

Her body couldn't stop shuddering as she walked away to go put the shovel back in the shed, looking at her monster, far from imagination and her worst of nightmares.

"You disgust me," Shayla spat at the priest. "I curse you!"

Like a coarse edge reverberating through her already jolted young soul, she felt his sudden slap across her face. Her balance leveled against the darkness, she stumbled to the wet and muddy ground atop the graves of "dead babies," as was her understanding of what laid beneath those graves. She suddenly felt the sting of a fresh cut under her chin which grazed the sharp edge of the gravedigger's shovel in her fall.

The damp patch of grass against her cheek and the smell of the dirt felt surreal, though only a further reminder of the horrific events of the night. Shayla's unmistakably frail and limp body stumbled back to its feet, revealing her face swollen from all the torment and crying hysterically, still bleeding from the cut under her chin. Her hair was soaked and muddied from the fall.

With a strange relief, there was an air of sympathy for her unknown, now buried soul. Though she could not better understand the night's circumstances, she knew the tragic experience from inside her had left her core. She felt inexplicably liberated. Free of anything inside her body that once belonged to him.

After the most heinous of acts to have befallen young Shayla, her feticide forever buried in the cemetery, the priest drove her back to his mother's house, where the nightmare all began. In the car, she wondered how many other young girls, before her, had been brought to the forbidden grounds for the same purpose of burying the priest's cruelty—and their unborn babies.

Back at the house of the priest, his mother cared for Shayla for a week before she was sent home to her family. As she was about to leave, the priest approached the still fragile girl, forever broken and apprehensive of his presence. He went down on one knee and held her by the hands.

"Listen to me sweet girl," he said. "What happened to you was only a dream, a very bad dream. You are totally fine and healthy to go home." Shayla became alarmed, as she pulled back, not trusting this demon in his priestly wear.

"You must never tell anyone about your dream," he urged. "People would never believe you. And your father especially will think very badly of you. You must never say anything to anyone. There will never be another bad dream. This I promise you. Now go on and do tell your parents you were a good girl and that I am ever so thankful you came to help me."

Shayla could only see the wicked truth in him. Not a "good" priest and a drastic polar opposite from his spotless image. Gone was her long-held regard, as had been of her family, about this community figure. The revered priest, who was also a published author, had garnered quite the enviable reputation among the locals. One would never surmise to the contrary. He was their celebrity. After all, he was known as the kind priest who would help the people of the village. *And so he did. Including helping himself to the young and innocent among his flock.*

Her parents were completely oblivious to what had taken place between their daughter and the venerated priest. Had they only known the truth.

On her way home, Shayla remembered when her father had asked him for help with some legal paperwork. One time when he came over to the house to speak with her father, she was scared, having already been violated by this cloaked monster. When the priest got there, he'd asked Shayla's father if she had been a good girl. Her father of course answered, "Yes."

How could this happen to her? How could she and her parents, devout followers of the priest, have become prey to the priest's blatant trap?

No longer a bad dream. But Shayla's very real life. A vile threat, the priest's words of "never tell" wreaked of the venom that had permeated her young soul. Now forever lost in some unknown tiny grave, along with the girl's innocence.

The nightmare would not be over until the priest was completely gone, Shayla contemplated. She had to rid the shame of her unfortunate past or she could not move on.

Lost and suicidal, at the incredibly young tender age of ten, she feared being judged and scorned for his horrifying acts upon her, despite being helpless at the hands of this predator.

Her chastity taken from her, she was out for revenge. Shayla knew what she had to do next. Kill the priest, the wretched vermin once inside her. Absolutely. And very soon.

She'd plot and would not rest until she had his blood on her hands.

CHAPTER 2

Veil of Secrets

Present day.

A risk far too great to take, Shayla could never let her guard down while trying to find herself in her new life—now a forty-something grown adult. She had escaped her homeland, the island, where her nightmarish past began as a young girl—only to leave her hurt beyond remorse. She could no longer take it anymore. With no time limit, the secret ate at her soul. When the opportunity came up for her to flee, she took it and never looked back. This was her chance to break away into a future that had nothing to do with where she came from. The deeply troubled Shayla had left it all behind. Her family. Her life. Her entire world. Making her journey to America was her only way toward redemption.

Shayla had endured so much pain and shame on the island back home since her youth, somewhere in Southwestern Europe, and she was quite ready to leave it all behind—the nightmare she had suffered under the hallowed disguise of the treacherous priest. Her torment was beyond what any young girl her age could handle. Shocked and emotionally tortured, with her faith forever shattered, she often wondered how a child could go through such a horrific experience.

In fear of her dark secret coming to light, Shayla became extremely savvy in creating the perfect façade where nobody could ever pick up on what had really happened to her, or what was going on inside her troubled mind. No one could ever know how she had lived through her adolescent years—as if her heart had been forever wedged with a knife. In her attempt to bury the past and muster through the pain, she lashed out her cries internally and silently. Shayla would play the song, "The Sound of Silence," repeatedly in her mind for many years. This ritual, in its own way, had served as a cathartic release of all she had endured.

She was in staunch agreement with the song's lyrics, "Silence, like a cancer grows." Her emotional silence over time also grew—before it ultimately erupted into an internal release, leading to her plan.

She had to escape the island where the heinous events of her youth, at the hands of the priest, had completely broken her innocent shell and emotionally destroyed her for life—*now a secret she would do everything in her power to conceal forever.* Her escape was only the beginning.

To create a fresh start in her new world was not really an issue for the resilient Shayla—it was erasing the memories of her past that haunted her daily. When she left the island, this meant more than just moving to a different country. She had to also establish a brand-new identity. She changed her name and started introducing herself as Emma in her *new life.*

To everyone she would encounter, she was Emma to them. Shayla had ceased to exist, in name only. Her past now buried, she continued to evolve into her adult years. Any painful memory had begun to fade over time into the vacuum of her violated core.

When the former Shayla left the island, she was determined to make a new life for herself at any humbled cost. She wanted to become entirely different, to be someone she could be proud of—which is when *Emma* was born. Recognizing her own strength with interpersonal skills and a driven intention to help people in pain, Emma put herself through school and started her own business as a massage therapist. All her efforts went exceptionally well. She was always at the office helping her clients, because they were her number one priority and a big part of her new world. She successfully grew her career—which meant more than just a career. It was her sanctum of safety, where she felt the most confident and assured. Knowing her clients trusted and adored her was her just reward. She gave them her heart and they loved her right back.

Living beneath her shroud of a reinvented life, devoid of painful history, Emma was cautious to never reveal her true identity for fear of judgement. She had strived for so long to release her past while working on her ultimate renaissance. Her escape from her former life now behind her, so far.

Before taking on the identity of Emma, she had faced many challenges that included learning a new language along with a new culture. Although thrilled about her new life, loneliness often set in, troubling the young Shayla. She would occasionally find herself in problematic situations when out looking for love at bars, where she quickly learned those places were not the most ideal for meeting the right people.

Along with her many disappointments and shed tears, moving to a totally unfamiliar new world at such a young age became a rude awakening she was not prepared for. Then one day, quite unexpectedly, she discovered comfort and love from a woman *[later revealed as Angelina],* who was twenty years older than Shayla. Unfortunately, their emotionally charged time together was short-lived. Shayla was so impacted by the loss of her cherished friend, it was then she had decided she would completely change her identity to a whole new character. From that point forward, her new name would be *Emma.*

On the surface, everything was fantastic for the reinvented Shayla, *now Emma.* Though not too tall, Emma had an athletic build. At first glance one might think she was a frequent gym enthusiast. She had long dark brown hair that she wore pulled back in a tight ponytail, creating more of an authentic look to her athletic appearance. Her natural perfectly shaped eyebrows framed her dark eyes. Her dark hair along with her accent, inspired most in contact with her to express her similarity to Natalie Wood, from when she starred in the iconic film, "West Side Story."

The more she rose in status within the community, that had accepted her as Emma, the greater the risk of her clients and friends discovering her hidden secret. She had to protect her entire new world that had become a haven to her. Those relationships could not be jeopardized in any way.

Despite all her efforts, she continued to fear her true past would be discovered someday. So, from religion to politics to relationships, Emma never discussed her personal views or experiences on anything with anyone.

She had become quite savvy at how she interacted with her circle of friends and clients. She did this extremely well. She would only discuss topics such as health and fitness, traveling, cooking, and other easy topical conversation. Through her efforts to engage and disengage, when needed, she remained mindful in her vigilance to protect her true identity. With a carefree personality she quickly learned how to simply smile and keep the conversation going. This trait, she was quite comfortable with.

As Emma, she had finally managed to build a new life of freedom where nobody could look into or even imagine her former life of shame. *Her new world and circle of friends could never know.*

The more she rose in status within the community, that had accepted her as Emma, the greater the risk of her clients and friends discovering her hidden secret.

Then... One day, a client appearing distressed, came to Shayla's office and confided about her concern with the welfare of her potentially troubled young daughter.

The client was distraught over her child's sudden refusal to go to her grandparents' house for their upcoming family summer vacation—something she had done every year since she was little.

Every summer, her daughter, Maddison, along with her older siblings, would visit her grandparents, aunts, uncles and all the cousins. However, this particular year, the daughter threw a temper tantrum leaving Emma's client shocked because she had never seen such outrage from her daughter before.

This scenario sounded eerily too familiar for Emma who desperately tried not to heave from a sudden anxiety attack.

Emma turned off the lamp, bringing darkness to the desk and the office around her. Another long workday was over, and she was thoroughly exhausted. From the moment she arrived in the morning to open the office, to the end of the day, she gave everything she had to her clients.

It was late spring. That meant the sun was out later, giving her enough time to do other things with her day after work. She was on her time now. A feeling that gave her a sense of reward. Maybe she would putter in the yard or go for a walk down by the creek.

Emma put on her light jacket. She locked the back door and turned off the front lobby lights. Then, while fishing through her purse for her keys, she saw a car turning into the office parking lot. In a frozen state, a twitchy panic raced through her as the car skidded to a halt.

Can they see me in the doorway, she wondered? If she was going to duck out of sight, she had to do it now.

Then a thought came over her. *Why was she so worried?* People came and went from her office every day. Emma tried to catch her rapid breath. She felt unusually eerie on this particular early evening. The sudden duress of seeing the vehicle pulling into her lot had triggered some deep-seeded wound.

Before Emma knew it, she heard voices. They were familiar voices. The car doors closed and a woman, followed by a young girl, hurried to Emma's office door.

It was Mrs. Bradley, Emma's client. She had her daughter, Maddison, with her.

Emma quickly opened the office door to let them in. She tried to smile as Mrs. Bradley turned, revealing a face twisted with frantic worry.

"Is everything alright?" Emma asked.

Mrs. Bradley shook her head. She was a kind woman and open to a fault. Whatever was on her mind, she was set to let Emma know.

Quickly turning her attention to the little girl, Emma hoped to get an actual response. Maybe something was wrong with her mother?

"Maddison?"

The little girl perked up. Her bright eyes looked around the familiar office as though she had never been there before. Her normally rosy cheeks seemed pale and her expression tired.

"Would you like to get settled in my office?" Emma gave her most comforting smile. "I have some new magazines. You may want to check them out."

Maddison asked her mother with an innocent look and Mrs. Bradley responded with a nod.

The little girl loved to read magazines, just like Emma had when she was young. A connection they always seemed to bond over.

Mrs. Bradley walked Maddison to the office and said: "We'll be just a moment, honey."

Maddison sat down in the office. Once Emma was satisfied that the little girl was busy reading the magazines, she pulled Mrs. Bradley aside in confidence.

"I'm just so worried..." Mrs. Bradley blurted out the words before Emma could inquire.

"Can I get you something? Coffee? Water?"

Emma dealt with stressed people all day. When they were out of sorts, usually something to drink was a good way to calm them down. But the worried mother waved her off. Then she produced a lavender handkerchief from her pocket and wiped her eyes.

"What's happening?" Emma tried to console the mother. "Please, tell me."

Mrs. Bradley drew a steadying breath. She closed her eyes and craned her neck for another view around the corner, into the office where Maddison happily read the newest issue of *Highlights.* Emma remembered the cover of the summer activity issue showed a group of kids playing on the water.

"Every summer Maddison goes to her grandparents," Mrs. Bradley began.

Emma nodded. She knew this was part of the Bradley family routine where they would take time away, usually once school got out, to visit their family. As far as she knew, Maddison loved visiting with her relatives, often talking joyfully about their big white house, their farm animals, and the sprawling front lawn.

As Mrs. Bradley continued to open up about her daughter's concerns, Emma suddenly started to feel queasy—triggering an instant flashback to her hidden past. Many thoughts and feelings poured through her as she struggled to keep a cool composure in front of her client.

The rush of emotions was beyond Emma's control as her concerns grew for Maddison's welfare. She became more anxious and wanted to tell Mrs. Bradley about her own traumatic events from when she was the same age as her daughter. Emma's long concealed events from her painful past were now as clear as day piercing through her mind. Nevertheless, she knew she had to stay calm and be professional.

Emma could not let her guard down. However, the more Mrs. Bradley talked about Maddison's plea to not go away for the whole summer, the more nervous and unhinged Emma became. Adding to the tension as her client asked for her advice, Emma began to sweat profusely.

"She lost it," Mrs. Bradley continued to speak.

"What do you mean, Mrs. Bradley?"

Overwhelmed with her own shaky nerves, barely able to control the wavering in her voice, Emma sat down in one of the lobby seats.

"My child screamed and yelled and was completely inconsolable."

A tantrum? Emma thought. That kind of behavior wasn't like Maddison.

"Is everything okay at home?" Emma asked before catching herself.

Mrs. Bradley nodded.

"What about school? Are you sure everything is okay?"

"Of course I'm sure," Mrs. Bradley replied. "I volunteer at the school. She loves it."

"Then what do you think it might be?"

"I don't know," the worried mother said, clasping her hands over her mouth. "Maddison is now just being stubborn and refusing to go. I don't understand it and I am really concerned."

Emma noticed Mrs. Bradley was not aware of the blatant signs Maddison was communicating—just like she had attempted with her own mother during the dark period of her youth. It didn't take long for Emma to realize that this was more than just a child throwing a tantrum.

"What are you two talking about out there?" said Maddison from the other room.

Startled, Emma nearly jumped out of her seat at the sound of the child's voice. Her palms were sweaty. She felt a rush of dizziness, suddenly weak, like she might pass out. Yet, she somehow pulled it together.

"Your grades in school," Emma chimed in as a buffer.

"Come on," she whispered to Mrs. Bradley. "Let's go talk to her and see what this is all about." Though on some subconscious level, without knowing more, she recognized the girl's trepidation to go visit her relatives all too well.

Emma noticed Mrs. Bradley was not aware of the blatant signs Maddison was communicating—just like Shayla had attempted with her mother during the dark period of her youth.

Though familiar in every way of Maddison's torment, Emma lacked the confidence to share her thoughts with the young girl—fearing if she opened up, this might backfire and potentially create a negative result if her client didn't believe her story. So Emma simply kept her composure and remained focused on being supportive.

From her own traumatic experience, Emma knew the signs of a child in distress all too well. She couldn't handle it anymore. The conversation with Mrs. Bradley had conjured unhealed wounds from her youth, as Shayla. She tried to diffuse her truth coming out by engaging Mrs. Bradley in conversation, along with getting Maddison to talk about her school and her pet cat named Fluffy.

Once Mrs. Bradley had calmed and Maddison seemed at ease talking with Emma about the cat, she noticed on her wristwatch that time had slipped away and she needed to get home to prepare dinner for her other older children.

Emma was relieved that, even though it was a close call, she'd managed to hide her explosive flashback. Soon after Mrs. Bradley and Maddison left, she grabbed her purse and keys and fled out of her office like a thief in the night escaping from a crime scene.

Emma drove the long way home. She wound through the open farmer's fields, past meadows shimmering in the sunset, over the river and down into the woods. The whole time she could not let go of thoughts about the disturbing meeting with her client and daughter Maddison. Her greatest concerns had come to pass. As she first suspected, Maddison Bradley had been molested. This was the first time Emma had experienced such a vivid flood of her own memories—in light of the whole Maddison revelation.

These emotions completely filled her, suddenly at the forefront of her mind's eye from her own traumatic escape in the lost decades before. The news from Maddison hit too close to home—*the old home Emma had left behind in her attempt to never relive the traumatic experience or the memory that haunted her.*

From the moment she heard that Maddison had burst into tears, the lock on her own internal safe broke, and like a dam, permeated her core and was no longer containable. The visit with Maddison had triggered all sorts of pain, shame, and anxiety she could not withstand.

The horror of those memories, as Shayla, had suddenly caught up with her new life, as Emma. Something she had fiercely protected—her secret and a hopeless life of long ago filled with dark, sad days when she felt lost and all alone. Those painful flashbacks no longer distant, were now clearly before her. Again…

The priest's rough hand on her bare thigh. His hot breath smelling of cigarettes, followed by his menacing look that said, "Don't speak. Don't you dare speak, little girl."

By the time Emma had started her drive, her skin crawled with newly risen memories she could barely force down long enough to complete her drive home.

It was near dusk when she pulled into her driveway. The air was warm and the last light of the day golden—though she felt none of the joy she usually did from the beautiful sight.

Once inside her home, Emma paced the kitchen. She tried to

occupy herself with cleaning up, tidying dishes, watering the plants in the window, but her mind was firmly locked into a tortured cycle of memory—as Emma couldn't shake off the exchange with her client's daughter.

"Mommy, don't make me go!" Maddison had screamed those exact words. Over and over again, and each time the little girl made her helpless plea, it forced Emma back to her youth and her true identity. *As Shayla.*

Maddison continued to plead to her mother with more urgency, her volume raised. Her alarming tone was enough to cause concern as she kept repeating, "Mommy, please don't make me go!"

Emma suddenly heard her own voice echo back from a time long before—in her own personal plea with her mother, deaf at the time to the horrors of what her daughter had gone through. "Mommy, please..." Emma would start.

Emma and Maddison were linked by more than their childhood love of magazines. She picked up the phone in a jittery hand and made a plan. She would call her best friend, Lauren. Trying to muster her strength, "Hello?"

"Hello? Who is this...?" Lauren's light and airy voice normally lifted Emma's spirits. Though not this time.

"It's me. It's Emma," she said with a scratchy throat.

"Oh dear." Lauren caught on right away. "What's wrong?"

"Can you come over?"

After hanging up from her call to Lauren, Emma wondered if calling her was the right thing to do. Fighting rampant thoughts of self-doubt, she suddenly lost the strength to talk openly with Lauren.

How was Emma to explain to her dear friend who she truly was? Not knowing what to do, she nervously paced her living room with thoughts of self-loathing. Negative thoughts that Emma believed had faded with time—suddenly resurfaced as feelings of self-hatred and permeated her core.

Will Lauren understand? Will she judge me? I am not the woman she thinks I am. I'm living a double-life in the shadows. Lauren will make me speak up. She may not want to keep my secret. I'm a pathetic soul. No one cares about me. I should never tell anyone who I really am. If I died tomorrow, they would read a fake eulogy. I am a lost cause. I can never face the truth. I'd rather live a lie and just carry the truth to my grave. I am unworthy and unfixable.

With a rush of more emotions eating into her soul, Emma began to cry hysterically. Her face buried in her hands, she screamed out, "I cannot bear the shame and judgment from others! I'd much rather hide in the dark and die in my own misery."

Thinking she'd made a mistake, Emma prepared to call back Lauren and cancel the impromptu visit with her trusted friend. But just then, her friend was already at Emma's house and rang the doorbell. As Lauren walked inside, much of Emma's angst started to fade away.

Lauren was soft-hearted and easy to talk to. In well-worn blue jeans and a soft maroon sweatshirt, she had her short, black, perfectly well-groomed hair tucked behind her ears and as always, her impeccable make-up emphasized her vivid light blue eyes. She was the kind of person that looked comfortable wherever she went, she spoke well and always showed interest in learning about other people's culture and interests.

Lauren had never judged Emma and the two of them had developed a trusting and amiable bond. The women had been best friends for many years. They met at the local gym, where Lauren was the owner and Emma was the front desk greeter to members. It was effortless for them to become the closest of friends, despite their age difference with Lauren being fifteen years older. She admired Emma's enthusiasm about living in America and the fact that she desired to learn English and the American culture.

Lauren would never forget the day when Emma had asked her to be taken to the bank so she could open a bank account. It was Shayla's first.

Lauren was happy to help Emma and asked her how much money she had saved up.

Emma's response was quick and without hesitation, "I don't know how much in total, but I have a green trash bag full."

Emma's excitement combined with a genuine sincerity made Lauren laugh for years to come.

They were a good balance for each other. Lauren was conservative and skittish, while Emma was wild and adventurous. The two friends had an unbreakable connection. They listened to each other all of the time. Emma learned to become more subtle, and Lauren learned to be more daring. The two inseparable women had often been called each other's sidekicks. Even at family and friends' gatherings, they were *jokingly* compared to as husband and wife.

As the two women sat across from one another in the living room, Emma tried to pick up on that feeling as if to try to borrow from it.

"What's the matter?" Lauren asked.

It was just like Lauren to get right to the point. Their brief phone call had likely stirred up her curiosity. Emma started to talk a bit about the late meeting with Maddison and her mother, but she felt frenzied relaying even the simplest facts.

Emma bit her nails and struggled making eye contact with her friend. As she relayed details of the little girl's sudden outburst, she had the sensation of being in two places at once. Her body was there, in her living room, across from her dear friend—however the rest of herself was elsewhere, raging against a tormented feeling of complete helplessness.

Emma reached the end of her story about the dilemma with the Bradleys. Lauren knew there was more to the story. She crossed her legs, gripped the arms of the chair, and looked at Emma.

"What's really the matter here?" Lauren prodded Emma with her unwavering gaze piercing into her dear friend.

"Lauren, I couldn't protect Maddison," Emma said, trying to conceal where her concern for the child was truly coming from.

"Of course, you couldn't. It's not your job."

"Lauren, I failed her."

"Emma..."

She shot Lauren a questioning, evasive look.

"Emma, I know you. If you could help, you would have done so."

"My heart," she struggled. "It won't let me open up to speak about it."

Lauren furrowed her brow.

"I'm struggling with these... these emotions, new ones, and I'm afraid to speak. I'm afraid Lauren that my anger is back."

Lauren looked confused. "What anger are you talking about?" Warm steady tears-soaked Emma's face as if a faucet had been turned on behind her eyes.

"I'm here for you, okay Emma? Whatever you're going through, I can help. But please, you must let me in."

Emma nodded.

"Emma, can you tell me what is troubling you, really?"

Emma began to open up. "There is a little girl I once knew," she drew a big breath. "And if I told you I cried myself to sleep every night thinking about her, would you believe me?"

Lauren's hand covered her chest. Her velvety blue eyes filled with shock.

Emma prompted again, "Would you?"

Lauren nodded. "Who is she? How old is she?"

"Would you believe me?" Emma felt rage consume her chest. "Would you?"

"Of course, I would. Yes! But you must tell me..."

Before Lauren could finish, Emma collapsed before her. Their exchange had reduced her to a frail and broken spirit. She dropped her head in her hands and let loose a torrent of pent-up emotions.

"I will tell you. She was hurt... actually so badly hurt, she was severely injured. She lived her life with her soul leveled at half-mast." Emma sobbed, trying to find the strength to look up at her trusted friend.

"Emma, what do you mean by she lived her life like that? Did she die? Tell me everything."

"Lauren, I thought she died. But she didn't. She's still alive, but she has been running from her past for so many years and today she suddenly reappeared. She's alive Lauren!"

Lauren interrupted her friend as she was rambling on and grabbed her by the shoulders. "Listen to me Emma. Who is this little girl? You must tell me now."

Emma grasped her small framed friend by the hand and pulled her closer. Her inner dam suddenly breaking, even more, she wept uncontrollably.

At that very moment, Emma blurted out, "Her name is Shayla! I will tell you her story from the very beginning."

CHAPTER 3

The Good Girl

Fifty years in the past.

The sun swept field gave way to the radiance of the season, spring, the favorite time of year for young Shayla, then a spry ten years of age. Her fanciful ways spirited along the fields as she picked the brightest flowers and filled her wicker basket. She couldn't wait to rush home to show her mother her floral finds of the day.

This was the happiest time for Shayla—her youth—pure, innocent, and unscathed. Looking back at this poetic period in Shayla's life is practically surreal, like a dream, taking her back to her small village in Portugal. It was the kind of community where everyone knew each other. This was where Shayla's parents had raised her together with her sister in the late '60s in a small farmhouse that offered resplendent views of the ocean from within the idyllic, manicured farmland. Beyond pristine, this was home for young Shayla, where everything was familiar, and she felt comfortable and safe.

During those times in that part of the world, it wasn't unusual for a plain, simple house to consist of a relatively spacious kitchen with two bedrooms, and lack of electricity or indoor plumbing. Shayla shared a bedroom with her sister. It had two small beds with handmade mattresses that were filled with straw, and adorned with handmade quilts. Similarly simple, but sturdy, the furniture somewhat filled the rest of their room and the house.

Her mother took extraordinary pride in her children's appearance, so Shayla's look mirrored that of the family home—modest, yet tasteful. She had a favorite dress, for instance, that was made of a soft blue and white fabric, laced with a pale blue ribbon around the neckline, sleeves and the bottom of the dress. Shayla also had a way she liked to keep her long dark waves in a bun that was lined with the same lace from her dress.

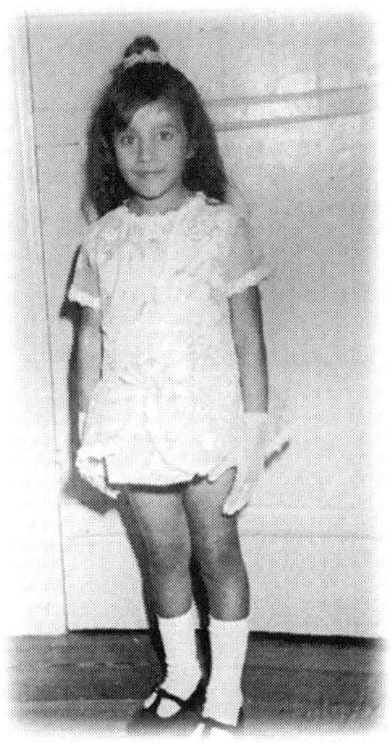

Young Shayla wearing her favorite dress. Only 6 years old, still a happy little girl (then) living with her parents and sister... Shayla was totally unaware of the looming violent rapes she would suffer only three short years later, by age 9, at the hands of her village priest (a hero in her parents' eyes who were oblivious to subjecting their daughter to a pedophile when they insisted, she take music lessons with him)... And then Young Shayla's nightmare began.

Everything was wonderful with her family during these happier times. Shayla and her sister shared a close bond; two nice girls from a lovely family.

As a child, Shayla's parents and her sister were her world.

She had an anxious side; something grounded in her deep curiosity, paired with her enthusiastic and sometimes rebellious streak.

Those traits rose to the surface in various ways. With an insatiable curiosity, Shayla wanted to know everything, so query she did, constantly asking questions. This part of her demeanor left her parents perplexed, if not frustrated, as they grew concerned over her exhibiting a pronounced independent streak.

Shayla was quite aware of her parent's frustration with her overriding personality. This led to her ignoring the house rules, cooking her own meals, growing her own flowers and making her own clothes—all of which she tried to do quickly and discreetly, so her parents wouldn't have to reprimand her.

Not only did Shayla know how to cook, she could also gut and clean chickens and fish before dinner. A somewhat puzzling dichotomy, as she loved animals and had a rather promiscuous cat. She would even spend hours outside pretending to be a veterinarian. And during times of loss, she would ensure the smallest of God's creatures received their proper burial.

Shayla was totally unaware of the looming violent rapes she would suffer only three short years later, by age 9, at the hands of her village priest.

Being outside as much as she was added to Shayla's rich complexion, making her naturally dark skin even darker. The locals would sometimes refer to her as "cockroach." Hardly a flattering moniker, this dubious endearment later affected her self-esteem.

To make her feel better, her mother, ever the nurturer, told her the people meant to call her "ladybug," since she was so cute. Perhaps Shayla picked up her active nature from her mother, who was also a hard worker.

In the summertime, she would take burlap sacks and weaved baskets full of cabbages or other vegetables to bigger nearby villages, using the town bus, to go selling them door-to-door. She would also use extra-large weaved baskets and fill them with all the fruit she'd picked the night before. She did this first thing in the morning, five days a week.

Together, Shayla and her mother loved to make bread. On the hot summer days, Shayla's mom would suffer a great deal from the heat, making her weak, so she would ask Shayla to get her some water.

Young Shayla enjoyed a close bond with her father as well. He knew all about hard work; he was a farmer and would work out in the fields all day. A simple man, he was stout and fairly strong with wavy hair and an arched right eyebrow that gave him a rather quizzical look. He lacked a formal education and could barely read at basic level. He wore a straw hat and the native albarcas shoes, as worn by most villagers.

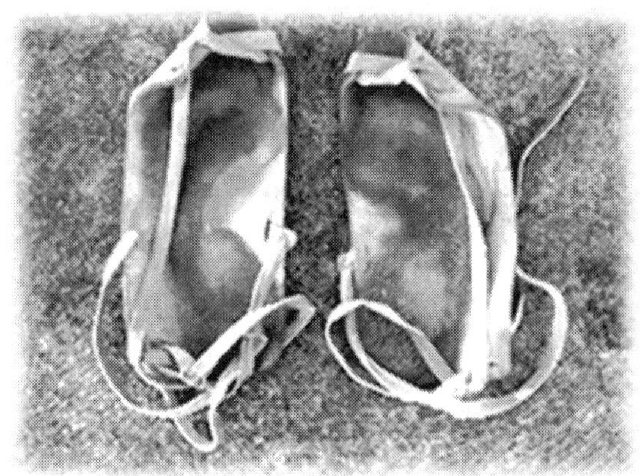

Albarcas Shoes

Shayla's father absorbed what he learned at his trade, and became quite good at it, then loved sharing it with his daughters. That worked for Shayla, feeding into her hyper curiosity. She was also quite intuitive when around adults, always listening, as she was able to keep up with everything that was being said around her.

"Father, look here. It has peanuts under there! Wow, that's how peanuts grow?"

"Yes, Shayla. Those are the peanut plant babies," he said. "They grow in the ground."

Shayla could go from an even-paced conversation with her father, where she was learning something, to another with her mother, leaving her baffled and distraught, as Shayla would not do as she was told.

"Dear God," said her mother. "I can't take my eyes off that child. Yesterday I asked her to get me just a couple of scallions, and she went and picked two. And when I asked her to go again and pick a couple more, she picked the whole row, and then asked me, 'Is this enough now?'"

"Did you punish her?" asked the father.

"No, I didn't punish her. But she did make me laugh when she turned around to go back outside."

"We need to guide her to be more focused and pay attention to the important things," the father suggested. "This will help her to not get distracted and do things wrong. Otherwise, we may as well let the chickens out of the coop because Shayla will destroy our crops in no time, just like the chickens would."

Shayla could go from an even-paced conversation with her father, where she was learning something, to another with her mother, leaving her baffled and distraught, as Shayla would not do as being told.

Shayla overheard her parents' conversation and felt terrible, but quickly forgot about it. Something she would learn to do, and become good at, was burying things that brought her pain. After hearing her parents, she promised herself that she would pay better attention to her actions and make her parents proud of her efforts. This was her new determined mindset.

Shayla's father knew of her love for nature and how she looked forward to his newest surprises for her. Like the time when he gave her an earthworm wrapped in a leaf, or another occasion when he brought a perfectly crafted bird's nest that had fallen from a tree, or even better, the first ripened fruit of the season.

Her parents came to see Shayla in a different light, realizing she was different from her sister, who was calmer and more settled. Still, the sisters had many interesting conversations while walking to school for thirty minutes every day. It was a single-room school, near the local church.

Shayla's family was very traditional in their Catholic beliefs, including being followers, almost to the point of being cultish, of the local priest at the church. They attended church on Sundays with their two daughters as they also tried to thwart her endless restlessness—ultimately taking their efforts, alas for young Shayla, to a point of no return.

Their Sunday routine became a challenge, as her parents would tell Shayla to either sit in the front or the back of the church. However, whenever mass started, Shayla became a walking commotion, as she would move up and down the middle aisle of the church and switch between sitting beside her mother or father. Sitting still in a quiet demeanor like her sister was not who she was.

The routine commotion at the church was only a prelude to the series of tragic events that would soon follow, to the detriment of Shayla where her welfare would suddenly be at stake. She didn't realize, then, that she was about to fall into a trap, and the priest's heinous grasp. Her spirited ways were on the brink of being upended and her life changed forever. A spiral that would all start with her father.

After mass ended one day, he approached the priest, though Shayla was hesitant to join her father and moved in the opposite direction. Having his daughter's best interests at heart, he simply asked the priest for suggestions, a solution, to help calm her mercurial ways.

The priest was quick to respond with an answer, and an offer, for her to sing in the choir. Though Shayla wasn't thrilled about the idea, her father told the priest that she'd be over the next day.

As the Sunday morning crowd dispersed, there was a bustle outside the church. One of the neighbors was all packed up to leave and started saying her goodbyes. Shayla and her father approached the neighbor to offer their farewell, as the departing woman—a younger Juliette—seemed distraught and tried to warn Shayla of... *Something.*

As Juliette hugged Shayla goodbye, she attempted to whisper discreetly into her ear, "Don't ever be alone with the priest, Shayla..." Jolted by Juliette's untimely warning, and before Shayla could process her words, their parting hug was suddenly cut short when her father reminded it was time to go.

CHAPTER 4

Painful Recall

Present day.

Emma was still reeling from her breakdown and revelation to her friend, Lauren. Coming forward to her, about Shayla, was something she had to do. Not opening up was no longer an option. She could not keep her concealed past to herself and not tell someone what happened. Her long-buried truth had to come out. She had to release the toxic secret that ate at her soul with each year that followed her nightmare, as Shayla. As she had started to tell Lauren, Shayla was still very much alive—including with all her demons. Emma let it all out, telling Lauren everything that happened to her back on the island under the horrific control of the priest. Though her breakdown and opening to Lauren was a beginning, it wasn't enough. Emma knew she couldn't stop there and had to continue finding her emotional freedom in other ways. She had to unbind herself from the traumatic cobweb that hindered her from truly letting go and moving forward in life.

As Emma grew older into her adult years, farthest away as she could from her youth and her past, *as Shayla,* the time that separated her self-emancipated *new life and identity* bared little consequence, or relief, from the horrific trauma endured when she was violently attacked by her old village priest. For all her efforts to forget and bury this dark period from her homeland, the pain and suffering was however forever wedged into her days, turned into years, that followed her escape to America.

The former home of happier times for a spry young Shayla had turned dark too soon in her childhood when she was still undeveloped and unworldly to fully grasp the unspeakable acts brought upon her. The priest had leveled her view and trust of people, including her very own self-effacing spiral decline, further compounding her struggle to move forward and past her nightmare. The padre's repeated molestation bore into her psyche and stunted her emotional growth as a woman—with her faith shattered forever.

For the modern-day Shayla, posing as Emma in her new life, this endeavor was not without its complications or setbacks. The harder she tried to bury her past, memories of the wretched priest continued to permeate her broken vessel and haunt her attempt at freedom.

Had she only been able to hear the words of warning from her long-lost childhood friend, Juliette, perhaps then little Shayla's tragic experience might have been avoided. She had always looked up to Juliette who was several years older and more like a big sister. Their moms were friends which was how the two girls met in those earlier years. Juliette had developed a protective bond and sweet affection for Shayla who she would babysit as a young child.

When Juliette was in her early twenties, she decided to leave the island forever. What most people didn't realize about her departure from the village was that it was truly her escape, from the priest, and her only way to get away from him. At the time of Juliette's embarked voyage, Shayla was about nine years of age. This was also the same time when her father wanted her to take up music lessons at the suggestion of their priest.

As it turned out, this would be a price she would later pay for the rest of her life. Deaf to Juliette's attempted warning, it would not be long before she, too, would fall prey to the monstrous priest following Juliette's departure—becoming the latest victim, and Juliette's replacement, for this devil in his priestly guise.

Shortly after the brief, short-circuited exchange between the girls on that somber day, Shayla would be brutally molested by the priest, devoid of any remorse, but emboldened instead by attacking the young and the weak. Shayla had been lured into the priest's evil web under the ruse of his pseudo music lessons.

Her one-time youthful shell had radically shifted from her friend's ill-fated words to ultimately being violated herself, beyond repair, to the point that she barely recognized her own reflection in the mirror—for all she saw staring back at her was a scared, fragile and hurt little girl who never came to terms, *and true healing,* from this ghastly torment of her past. She no longer believed there was good in the world.

As if Shayla's childhood had not endured enough trauma caused by the priest, she further felt abandoned by her own father—who could not see, or recognize, the torment befallen to his daughter under the heinous control of the priest. Her father, the onetime true love and protector she had ever known, was forever lost.

The harder she tried to bury her past, memories of the wretched priest continued to permeate her broken vessel and haunt her attempt at freedom.

As Shayla evolved into her young adult years, though only physically as still emotionally scarred by the priest, she would later befriend her newest love and protector—an older adult woman named, Angelina. It was also then when Shayla had decided to make a radical shift in her self-identity, not only to herself—but to the world—as altering to her assumed name and persona, *as Emma.* The change represented so much to her in moving forward with a new lease on life alone. The emancipated Emma would endeavor to lose any association to her former existence and torment, *as Shayla.* She never wanted to look back at her past, ever again.

Even in her breakdown revelation to Lauren, though she started to share what happened to her, as Shayla with the priest, including her following years with Angelina, she didn't quite tell her *everything*. An even more intrigued Lauren, trying to piece together Shayla's mysterious life, would later prompt, "Tell me more about Angelina and how does she play into the picture?"

In her current make-shift adult existence, as Emma, for all her trials at burying the past, and while she was able to mute the memory, on her infrequent good days, the reflection from her past had not entirely gone away.

In the beginning, following the repeated and violent rapes by the priest, it became evermore a challenge for the still young Shayla to accept or forgive herself, despite these dreadful episodes being out of her control.

Though not her fault and she did nothing wrong, she didn't know who she was anymore. She remained scathed and horrified, hating to look at her shamed self, as internal demons ate at her damaged soul.

As an adult Emma, for all her attempts to look beyond her past, she kept seeing her young abused essence—the inner-child who never truly healed. No matter how long ago, it was still never long enough for Shayla, turned Emma, to truly forget. And forgive, *including herself.*

Thinking she could outrun her past, she had migrated many miles far away from her small village in Portugal, where the nightmare happened. However, memories of the priest continued to haunt her, day and night, even in her new home of America. When Emma later discovered the priest had passed away, she wished she could have taken away his last breath. She lived with vengeance in her heart. If he'd never raped her, she believed she would have been a better person. She would not be cruel to people who tried to show her love and acceptance—those she had otherwise pushed away, as holding the priest accountable for her actions. To shun people became a reactive protective measure, her shield of armor. *No one would ever hurt her again.*

Despite being protective, she would continue to work on herself.

Emma kept trying to not be *that person* anymore. She had grown tired of being tired and running from her past. She didn't want to blame the world, *anymore,* for what had happened to her. It was time to calm her pent-up fury. She knew she owed it to herself to create a better journey forward that was surrounded with positivity. And no longer the negativity that held her back.

Over time, she became better at it—moving forward and embracing the value of her newly evolved life toward better days.

One way her self-work *worked,* where she found solace and relief, was by going on long road trips surrounded by nature. These drives helped to soothe her soul and replenish a new lease of hope for the improved Emma, as further reinforcing and enriching her days. She looked forward to simply losing herself along a newest traverse on a road that spoke to her—a welcome metaphor *driving* her open heart forward to a feel-good, better place. *Her recovery roads became well-traveled and helped her to heal.* So she would try to go on new road trips as often as she could.

Through Emma's older adult life, the span of time since her youth had started to fade into the background. She taught herself how not to look at or focus on the past, and was grateful for the time that had passed. It helped her to forget, even somewhat, so she could put her mind on other things that contributed to positivity—the only thing she would allow anymore. Whether it was through her work or in new found relationships. She learned to recognize, trust and cherish these opportunities. Her clients and friends became her new inner-circle of faith—her extended family.

Emma also started to apply the practice of manifestation into her life, where she would *will* into her days the outcomes she desired. Infused into her daily habits, this practice started to work for her where things just started to click, even more. Then one summer day she received the call.

She had made earlier plans to go on her newest road trip with the destination unknown at the time. She was fine not knowing or planning further into her drives. It was more important for her to just get on the road, *and go anywhere.* She also enjoyed going on these excursions with a companion. Usually, a girlfriend who shared the same enjoyment as she did on these drives, where they could just drive together for hours on end in their new adventure on the road.

Emma's latest planned trek with a friend would go for a week, but the friend had to cancel due to an emergency. Unfettered, Emma was determined to find a replacement road companion who would take the weeklong trip with her.

The idea was to start driving on a Monday morning, for a few days straight, while stopping only to gas up, eat and catch some sleep at local hotels when the night set in. As she began contemplating her approach and who she would ask next to accompany her road trip, her phone suddenly rang.

"Hello," said Emma.

"Hi, is this Emma? The same Emma who worked at Defense Technologies in the late 1980s?"

"Yes, it's her," responded a guarded Emma. "Who's this?"

"Emma, I am so glad to find you," exclaimed the strange voice on the other end of the line. "This is Mary. Do you remember me? We worked together at Defense Technologies many years ago, when we used to also share recipes."

Emma's heart racing, she replied, "Yes, I do remember you, Mary! How are you? What's going on?"

"Well Emma, it's the strangest thing. I was talking to my next-door neighbor about how I used to know a vibrant young lady who seemed to come from the same island as her, my neighbor. I described you to her and mentioned your name, Emma. And my neighbor then suddenly flipped out, almost went into shock, saying she might know you and had to find you. So she and I have been on a hunt ever since. You wouldn't believe that after many phone calls to former acquaintances from our old work, we were able to finally track you down when someone said they had your current contact information. I mean, Emma, what were the odds?! Plus, as I was sharing more about you with my neighbor, she corrected me saying she believed your real name was Shayla. Is that right? Is that truly you, Emma? I mean, Shayla?"

Trying to contain her excitement and flurry of emotions, with an inkling of a hunch, Emma quickly asked Mary, "What is your neighbor's name?"

"Her name is Juliette. Does that sound familiar? She said she knew you when you were a young girl and that she used to babysit you back on the island."

As if a phone drop moment, without the phone actually dropping, Mary's words combined with hearing Juliette's name sent Emma into shock—as surreal images floated across her mind's eye of her last shared moments and interaction with a then distraught Juliette, recalling how she appeared before Emma would never again see her childhood friend.

Within that brief moment, Emma further recalled how Juliette was trying to warn her about something with the priest. Although she never quite made that connection of her warning, *until now.*

Her recollection further illuminated, Mary's call had triggered Emma's memory of her experience when she was attacked by the priest and it was already too late, then, at the hands of her predator. She further recalled how she would later hear local rumors from her old village about how Juliette had become the priest's sex slave, his known mistress and lover for many years, before she ultimately left the island. Jolted back to the present by Mary's call, like a desperate prayer being answered, it felt like a dam suddenly rushed through Emma as she quickly put greater meaning into the *deeper connection* she truly shared with Juliette—that stretched far beyond just a long-lost friendship. Mary's preemptive call of that day touched Emma's core at the most profound level.

All was starting to make sense and come full circle for the former Shayla in her assumed adult role, *as Emma.* Shook back to her conversation with Mary, as still trying to process her emotions, she was further taken aback by how Juliette happened to be the next-door neighbor of her former co-worker. *What were the odds?*

"Hello, Emma! Are you still there?"

"Yes, Mary!" The dazed, yet gleeful Emma returned. "I'm still here!"

"Oh good, I started to panic there for a moment, considering all we went through just to find you. I thought we dropped the call. I'm so glad you're still there, and that we *finally* found you! The real you, Emma! I mean, Shayla, of course. Well, you know what I mean. I'm just so excited, as I hope you will understand. And I know Juliette will be excited too!"

"It's all good, Mary," comforted Emma. "I'm so glad you called. What were the odds, right? That you just happen to be neighbors with my old childhood friend, Juliette."

"This is wonderful to hear, Emma, I mean Shayla," fluttered a gasping Mary. "So, let's do this. I would love to have you come over for dinner here. And I will also invite Juliette to join us. She showed such interest in finding you, as she further recalled you being a 'fantastic little girl,' *her words.* And for many years she had wondered how you were. So, what do you think? We can surprise her!"

"Yes, absolutely Mary. That is a great idea. Thank you for your sweet and thoughtful invitation. I would love to come over. It will be so nice to reunite with Juliette again after all these years. And let's definitely keep it a surprise!"

After they hung up, Emma was so overcome with gratitude to receive Mary's sudden call, as she thought back to all the years it had been since they worked together. Something was finally starting to make sense in Emma's strange upended day that began when her road trip companion had cancelled.

As if a phone drop moment, Mary's words combined with hearing Juliette's name sent Emma into shock...

Mary's words, combined with hearing Juliette's name, sent Emma into shock...

All was so perfectly timed for the former Shayla who had continued to search for healing from her past. She knew reconnecting with Juliette would mean a way forward for *both* of them. She was trusting in the process and embraced the magic of her day. A new hopeful Emma now couldn't wait for her reunion with Juliette. She really believed this visit would mark a pivotal new beginning for yet her newest journey toward redemption.

Right then, Emma planned to ask Juliette to come along on her road trip when she would see her at Mary's home. She knew the drive together would help to mend a way forward to forgiveness, while finding compassion and releasing shame.

The day Emma had longed for had finally come. It was the evening she would be going to Mary's home for their planned dinner and surprise visit with Juliette. Leading up to this moment, Emma had grown nervous as the day for the dinner got closer. Filled with angst, thoughts of uncertainty rushed through her and before she knew it, she was standing at Mary's door. With a steady hand she rang the bell.

A warm and beaming Mary opened the door and welcomed Emma inside with open arms. Tense at first, Emma tried to conceal her emotions and acted like all was fine. She took a seat at the dinner table with Mary and they waited for Juliette to arrive. Mary started some small talk with her, sensing Emma's tension, and prompted her with questions to help break the ice. She asked Emma many questions about her personal life and what she had been up to in the years since they worked together. Though on such matters, Emma's long-guarded domain, she steered clear from any detailed discussion.

An ever-private person in her assumed identity, as Emma, she kept her affairs to herself and would only talk in general terms. It also helped for her to change the topic of conversation to Mary's beautiful home, such as complimenting her décor. Their chat then shifted to one of their long-held favorites; recipes of choice.

A few minutes later, the moment Emma had been yearning for was here. There was a knock on Mary's front door as Emma's heart began to race. She became even more nervous wondering if Juliette had shared with Mary anything about their haunted past. When

Juliette entered, Emma's heart melted seeing her standing inside Mary's home.

"I would like to *reintroduce* you to an old dear friend to us both," started Mary.

The surprise worked and Juliette was thrilled to see her old childhood friend who she would call, "my sweet little girl." Overcome with joy, Juliette burst as seeing who she recognized as Shayla standing right before her.

"Oh my God! Let me guess... Is that you? *Shayla!* My childhood friend from the village. I used to babysit you," exclaimed Juliette.

"Yes, it's me," cried out Shayla, losing all semblance to her Emma persona. "It is so good to see you again!"

Both teary-eyed, the two women quickly hugged with a long, tight and unbreakable hold. It felt like *coming home* for the two, now adult, women and cherished friends who were overwhelmed with joy to see each other. They sat down at the dinner table and began to exchange memories of good times, and not so good, from their shared past. Their chatter evoked a resilient bond in the heart of Mary's home. A connection that was devout and solid, no matter the span of time that had elapsed since their parting on the island.

Breaking down her earlier barriers, Shayla *came out* and was quite present in her exchange with Juliette. She felt comfortable and free with her old friend, and knew in her heart that Juliette was the friend she had longed to confide in about all that had happened to her. The enamored women so enjoyed seeing each other and continued to chat it up throughout Mary's dinner, losing themselves as the evening hours carried on. Recognizing they had lost track of time, they knew it was time to leave. They all said their goodbyes, as Shayla and Juliette exchanged phone numbers.

The next day Shayla made good on her plan. She called Juliette and asked if she would like to join her for a road trip to Canada. Juliette didn't think twice and was happy to be part of the trip. Beyond the long drive and escape with her old friend, Shayla's true intentions were far greater. The reunion and excursion with Juliette held profound consequence for her. It symbolized a new opportunity for healing and closure of their horrid past under the clutches of their treacherous, albeit late priest.

Everything happens for a reason and this reunion was meant to be, thought Shayla. She was so grateful to have reconnected with Juliette at the right time—to finally turn over this chapter of her life, for good, and to be done with her pain and shame. Juliette represented the threshold forward to the other side of that release.

CHAPTER 5

Unholy Fucking

Fifty years in the past.

When a girl reaches nine years of age, she experiences body changes that can inspire curiosity and anxiety at the same time, especially if she doesn't know what to expect or what is normal.

Alas for young Shayla, this was the time of discovery of another kind. One turned into a real-life nightmare all too soon in her early growth and physical development. At only the tender age of nine, the nefarious priest had begun to commit the unthinkable upon her tiny little frame with his violent and repeated rapes. He would turn Shayla, still just a child then, into a sex puppet under the control of his physical might, his will and his vile threats. She would quickly learn how to internalize her fear and pain into an altered state of numbness, a seamless detachment, as her small body became an empty vacuum devoid of any feeling. This became her buffer and only shield, her emotional survival, to simply get through the dark moments of what was being done to her by the priest.

Doing as told, she obeyed this revered village Samaritan—the supposed good priest. Though behind his priestly garb laid a predator in wait. He thought nothing of preying on the young loyal subjects from his church; all while maintaining the utmost trust and a spotless image in the eyes of the parents. The priest could do no wrong in *their* eyes. Little did they know the priest was truly a monster, evil in every way, who would not think twice to victimize their own. Such as young Shayla, who would soon become his newest sexual victim and slave.

As Shayla started to smart against the priest's early advances, the time before being cornered when she would succumb to her ultimate and vicious fate at his evil hands, she would make it a habit to hide from the priest in the woods, spending hours there as she pretended to be a fairy in what she deemed her big great garden surrounded with the prettiest tiniest flowers, and where the birds also became her pets.

Her made-up menagerie and dreamscape became her safe haven for a short while as she tried to prolong her escape from the priest for as long as she could—until she couldn't anymore.

She knew all too well, as had become the pattern, that once in his grips he would thrust his repulsive largesse upon her tiny frame, emboldened even more and shouting, "Cry little cockroach," as he continued to force himself upon her frail form and broken soul. This became a regular cat and mouse exercise for Shayla during her every and repeated attempt to avoid the priest, before being caught. And she would, get caught. Again, and again. With each catch, the priest would break her once more.

There were no cockroaches in Shayla's imaginary garden, where no one could hear her plea for help. Instead, she would close her eyes during the priest's attacks as she pretended to be walking through the woods collecting wildflowers to bring home for her mother's table. This internal escape became like a slideshow in her mind's eye as she kept her eyes closed through the rapes. Little Shayla's *episodic escape* helped, somewhat, to take her attention off what the priest was doing—first with her tiny hand, then to her virgin body.

Her garden interrupted, he would force himself even more upon her tiny form, as her throat tightened and she gasped to be released from her monster. She would go back to visions of picking flowers, her internal refuge and only way to deal with the very real physical nightmare she suffered as being violently molested by the priest.

It was those heinous rapes that would lead young Shayla to the cemetery one rainy night with the priest to *release* what he had bore into her—and ultimately into a tiny baby grave.

On that gloomy night, echoes of her loud scream from the painful release of her aborted baby permeated the hallowed grounds. With her wail she dropped the unborn soul into the small grave she had dug up for that ill-fated purpose. Far from a nasty lucid dream, the events of that night were quite real—as were all the other dreadful nights that had led to this darkest moment in Shayla's life.

Before the attacks, nine-year-old Shayla had started to sing at her local church choir with other parish participants. Gifted with a good voice, she took great pride in being able to sing with the older choir members. She further enjoyed doing bible readings during Sunday mass. Her voice was clear and she always looked up between paragraphs of the readings as she had been instructed.

She was quite proud to be part of the choir group and always attended practice, which became once a week in the wintertime. The choir would meet up to practice their songs. Then after practice, the parish priest would drive all choir members to their homes, including those who lived further away. When everyone would pile into his car, young Shayla would always end up sitting on someone's lap because she was so small. Her home was the closest to the church, and if the priest dropped her off first, she would have been home before anyone else. Though he would always drive past her house and circle back to drop her off last. At first, Shayla was happy to go for the longer ride, as it was not very often that a child had the opportunity to ride in an automobile with a group of adults.

Then one rainy evening, the priest had everyone in his car while he smoked a cigarette that hung from the side of his mouth. He dropped off everyone from choir practice at their homes, and when he started to drive away from the last drop-off, he reached over to the back seat with his hand looking to touch Shayla's leg. She pressed herself as far as she could against the car door behind the driver's seat, but he could still reach.

He stroked her legs up and down a few times before he commanded her, "Move over to the middle of the seat."

"No," said Shayla. "I'm just fine here."

"Come on over to the middle," said the priest with a soft encouraging voice. "Don't be afraid, I just want to see you better."

"No, it's okay!" said Shayla, pressing her body even harder towards the car door.

Once they got to Shayla's house, the priest stopped the car and said, "It's raining, jump over to the front seat and wait here until the rain stops."

He reached over to where she was in the backseat, and before she had a chance to open the car door and run out, he pulled her towards the middle of the backseat. Facing forward with a crack of the front driver's window opened, the priest lit a cigarette with his left hand while he held Shayla on the seat with his right hand. He did not move his hand up or down, just left his hand on her knee area with a soft grip to let her know she was not free to go. Shayla was confused and unsure of what to expect as she had never been alone with a man in a car like this. The priest continued to hold Shayla by the knee with a soft grip leaving one finger available to rub her skin in small circular motions. Shayla pulled away, and the priest grasped her knee using a slight grip and said, "Not yet, Shayla, it's still raining, you have to wait."

"But I want to go home. My parents are waiting for me. I can run in the rain..."

The priest finished smoking the cigarette and threw the lit tip out the window as he turned to address Shayla. "Go ahead home. I only held you here because of the rain. Your parents would be terribly upset if you got sick by walking in the rain."

Shayla slid to the side of the seat and quickly opened the car door, jumped out and ran home as fast as she could, never looking back to see the priest who was still parked in his car. Though scared and confused, Shayla never told her parents the priest had touched her leg and grabbed her knee, pinning her in his car.

That night, Shayla couldn't sleep as she thought about the priest's unexpected actions toward her. She wanted to tell her mother, but didn't want to make her mad if she had ended up walking home in the rain. *Instead, Shayla decided to never tell anyone.*

The following week when it was time to return to choir practice, the members walked to the church and stopped by Shayla's house. Because she was so little, they assured her mother she would be safe to join them along their walk. With her okay, they all continued to walk together the rest of the way to the church.

Once the choir practice was over, again the approximate six members who needed to be driven home all piled into the priest's car and the drop-offs began. The priest went the usual route, conveniently driving right past Shayla's house and dropping everyone off at their homes first. Then on the way back the priest once again reached over to the back seat looking for Shayla's leg. Shayla moved over to the far side near the door, this time behind the passenger seat making it more difficult for him to reach her. When he noticed that she was sitting on the other side and not behind him, he suddenly stopped the car on the side of the road. He turned around to look at her and commanded, "Jump over to the front seat. Now!"

"Why?" she asked.

"Because you can sit in the front seat, like a big girl."

"No, I don't want to sit in the front seat. I just want to go home."

"I'll drive you home for sure, but it's still early."

This time Shayla quickly opened the car door and ran out as fast as she could and hid in the bushes. It was dark out and she was so tiny, she thought he would not be able to find her unless he had a flashlight. She heard him come out of the car and call her name, "Shayla, come on out of there. Don’t be silly. I am not going to hurt you in any way. I will drive you home. I promise."

In her attempt to keep hiding further into the bushes, she inadvertently made a sharp noise. The priest heard it and walked directly to the spot of the sound. There he found Shayla. He reached down and grabbed her by the hair, pulling her out of the bushes. He then held her by the arm and forced her back into the car; to the front seat this time.

Once inside, he insisted, “Stay still or I will tell your father that you misbehaved.”

He then went around the driver's side of the car, lit another cigarette and began driving towards Shayla's house. While he was driving, he reached over to where Shayla was seated next to him and touched her legs. This time he reached between her inner-thighs as his hand scaled deeper in toward her crotch.

He queried, "Do you have hair there yet?"

She did not respond.

He tried again, even more forceful this time. “I asked, do you have hair there?”

Without another word from either one, he grabbed her small skinny inner-thigh with more force. "I don't know," she whimpered, hoping if she gave him some answer maybe he would leave her alone.

When Shayla was first introduced to the act of sex, it happened quite innocently during the time when she and her mother had gone to visit a friend. Her son had returned home from the Armed Forces. It was a big deal for him to come back after a four-year deployment to Angola, as part of fighting for his mother country. Shayla's mother had made it a plan to visit the woman, while her other daughter stayed home reading and crocheting. Shayla's sister could focus for extended periods and would make the most beautiful doilies and clothes by hand.

Shayla quickly asked her mother if she could go with her to the friend's home, to which the mother allowed. When they got there, the young man was not home, but his mother was and welcomed Shayla and her mother with open arms. Shayla was always looking for something to read. There was a mobile library that came around the village once a month, allowing each child two or three books a month. Shayla would have her rationed books read in no time. She would also try to read her sister's books from the mobile library. Shayla had learned how to read when she was in the first grade because her sister, who was three years older, had taught her how.

While he is driving, he reaches over to where Shayla is seated next to him and touches her legs.

When they arrived at the home of her mom's friend, Shayla quickly asked if the lady had any chores to be done. Shayla was told her son's room needed to be cleaned and the bed needed to be made. Asking Shayla to make her son's bed and clean his room provided some alone time between the two adult women to have a conversation without Shayla in the room asking questions or eavesdropping on their chat.

Shayla knew exactly where to go to clean the young man's room. When Shayla walked into the room, she made the bed, picked some items off the floor, and then proceeded to sweep the floor just like how her mother had taught her to do.

As she bent down to sweep under the bed, she noticed a magazine on the floor. She instantly dropped the broom and picked up the magazine, quickly opening and flipping through the pages. With her big brown eyes as wide as can be and unable to move, Shayla was suddenly struck with horror for the first time in her life as she looked through the book. It was a hardcore pornography magazine filled with specific explanations about what the act of "fucking" was.

Shayla had heard the word "fuck" many times before, but only knew it as a word to say when mad at something or having an argument with someone. Observing the shocking images in the magazine, she was amazed by how big and hard a man's penis could be as going into a woman's vagina. She also had no idea that adults could have hair in that part of the body. She continued to flip through the pages, astonished to learn more about "fucking," as she saw various adults fucking on different pages. One thing all the men had in common was their big and hard penises.

Shayla's mother and her friend noticed Shayla had been gone for a while and had become quiet. They called out to her, *"Shayla!"* Her heart pounding, body shaking and still riveted by the contents of the magazine, she ran to the kitchen where the ladies had been talking. Though she evoked an air of guilt, the ladies had not noticed Shayla's terrorized eyes and quivering body.

Shayla's mother asked if she was done cleaning the room and she said it was almost done, with the bed made, and she was just sweeping the floor. The ladies nodded for her to return to the room and finish so they could continue with their chat. Shayla ran back to the son's room. She picked up the magazine and continued to look through more pages.

Shayla's mother wore many hats in her role as a homemaker. She was always busy cooking, cleaning, and during harvest time the mother and her two girls would help out with the crops. Her mother was a fantastic cook. Shayla and her sister always helped with all the house chores.

Shayla's mother would say, *"Rules to keep a good house and make a great meal: pick up your dirty laundry from the floor, keep your beds made, and your dishes always cleaned. As for cooking, add garlic, onion, salt, and pepper and you will always have a delicious meal."*

Everyone in the house would wear church clothes along with their church shoes, as her mother would make sure on Sundays that only church clothes would be laid out on the family beds for that sole purpose. Once they would return home from church, the girls would have to change into their play clothes if they wanted to go outside.

Shayla's mom would contract the local seamstress to come to their house every month so all dresses and undergarments could be made for her and the two daughters. Shayla loved it when the seamstress would come to sew their clothes, because the mother would make special food. Shayla's job was to thread all the needles, so the seamstress didn't have to put on her eyeglasses to see the eye of the needle and waste time trying to thread the needles.

Shayla had a line of needles with long thread always ready for the lady, and by doing this, she would listen to entire conversations between her mother and the seamstress. Those chats consisted of local gossip that Shayla was not allowed to take part in. This was when Shayla had also learned more about adult conversations—the time when she would learn new words and new things typically said or done by adults. One such conversation was started by the seamstress as whispering to Shayla's mother, "Did you hear what happened to the woman who lives in the brown-colored house?"

"The last thing I heard was that she was caught fucking the guy next door, you know the uncle of the young couple that lives on the hill," replied Shayla's mother.

"Oh yes, she was caught fucking him in the shed, then she was next seen going to the big lady with the whiskers."

"She went to the whiskers lady's house?"

"Yes, she did. And that night she laid a soft egg."

Caught up with the conversation between her mother and the seamstress, Shayla pretended to be threading the needles as she anxiously waited to find out what happened at the woman's house that caused the girl to lay a soft egg.

The next day Shayla had asked her mother if she could go visit her friend, the neighbor's daughter who was older than her. She purposely wanted to see this friend as she knew all about adult conversations. Shayla had never been so intrigued and curious to find out what was meant by how a woman could lay a "soft egg."

Shayla's mother permitted her to go to the friend's house. She walked over and could not wait to ask her questions. When she got there, some younger children were around, closer to her age. But Shayla was on a mission to go right inside where the oldest sister was, who was most likely cooking or cleaning the house with her mother. When she saw her friend, Shayla quickly asked, "What is meant when the lady who lives on the hill fucks the man who lives next door, then she is seen going to the lady's house with the whiskers, and then lays a soft egg?" The practically out of breath Shayla continued to prompt the friend, "What does this all mean?"

Almost falling to the floor, at first in disbelief, Shayla's friend was caught off-guard by the anxious and inquisitive Shayla with her baffling line of questions.

With a big smile, her friend responded, "Sweet girl, you are too curious and too cute for me not to tell you. Even though I think you are too young to be asking such questions, I believe you should still learn, so this never happens to you." The friend then grabbed Shayla by the hand and pulled her to the other room where they sat on a bed.

Her friend continued, "Shayla, do you know what fucking is?"

"Yes, I do. I saw a magazine that showed how a man and a woman fuck. And I even read the whole thing," said Shayla, proud to be so young and know more than kids her own age.

"All right then, the woman who lives on the hill was caught fucking with the young couple's uncle who lives next door..."

"I know," said Shayla with great enthusiasm.

"Let me explain, they are not married. They were fucking and the lady from the hill got pregnant."

"She got pregnant from fucking one time?"

"Well, we don't know how many times she fucked the man next door. But yes, you can get pregnant from having sex only one time."

"But only married women fuck their husbands."

"No, there are many women who fuck that are not married. They are called 'putas' and some even charge money. Those who charge money are called prostitutes."

"Prostitutes?"

"Yes, they charge money to fuck?"

"Does fucking hurt? In the magazine, I saw the man's cock was very big and it went in the woman's vagina all the way. The woman had her mouth open and her eyes closed."

"You are way too young to understand fucking, my sweet little girl. When you get older, you will understand," said Shayla's friend, trying to cautiously address Shayla's questions without getting into many details.

She continued, "Going back to the soft egg..."

"Oh yes, please tell me more about how a woman can lay a soft egg."

"Do you know that big woman who lives near the church with whiskers on her chin?"

"Yes, I do know her. My mom and I go there to sell fruits and vegetables all the time."

"All right then. She is a woman who learned how to perform

abortions in her house."

"What are abortions?" Shayla asked tentatively.

"An abortion is when a woman gets pregnant, but decides not to keep the baby. There is a procedure that can be done where it causes the woman to abort a pregnancy. And along with that, her baby..."

"Is that why it's called an abortion?"

"Yes, an abortion is a pregnancy that gets aborted, meaning it comes out of the vagina before it's time."

"How do you know if you're pregnant?"

"Shayla, do you see your mother wash cloths with blood on them every month?"

"Yes, I do. She puts the cloths in her underwear, and my mother says it's that time of the month again. Every woman has it."

"All right, so you know a woman has that time of the month. However, when you are pregnant, you don't have that time of the month anymore. It just stops. And that's when a woman knows if she is pregnant."

"So then, is that what happened to the woman on the hill? She didn't have her time of the month, and then she went to see the lady with the whiskers who did an abortion at her house."

"Yes, that's what happened."

"How did she do an abortion?"

"She inserted a long sharp wire into the vagina, then pokes at her insides until the abortion is completed."

With her eyes opened wide, Shayla was proud to be learning all this adult information as she further prodded her friend for more. "So how do you know this? Did you have an abortion?"

"No, my sweet girl, I didn't have an abortion. But I know someone who had one done."

"Do all women who fuck men they're not married to, have to have an abortion?"

"No, Shayla. Sometimes when women who are not married become pregnant, they can choose to have their baby. However, those women are typically outcast and are considered putas. They don't go to church and no man will ever want to marry them."

"What happens to their babies when they are born?" Shayla

continued to inquire.

"Their babies are considered bastards."

"What is a bastard?"

"A bastard is a baby who is born out of wedlock and doesn't have a father."

"Can a woman have a baby bastard without fucking a man?"

"No, Shayla. A woman always needs a man to have a baby. But if she is not married, the baby becomes a bastard because the father is not the woman's husband."

"I understand now, but what about the soft egg that she laid?"

Shayla's friend busted out laughing saying, "The soft egg is an expression that people say when a woman has an abortion because it is the fetus and tissue that comes out of the vagina. And it is soft."

"What's a fetus?"

"A fetus is when the baby starts to develop inside the woman's belly."

"Where does the soft egg go once it is out?"

"Normally women who have an abortion bury the fetus in the ground."

"Do they have a funeral?"

"No, Shayla. When a woman has an abortion and lays a soft egg... they don't tell anyone. Some women have even gone to the cemetery at night, dug a hole and gave their soft egg a proper place to decompose."

Shayla's friend suddenly realized this conversation with her little friend had gotten too deep and serious for Shayla to process.

"Now sweet girl, go on home and play with kids your age. Don't worry about a woman laying a soft egg and don't let your mother know you learned all this from me because she will be mad at both of us."

Shayla left the friend's house deep in thought, with still more to be understood. *So much to process.*

As if the sequence of events leading up to Shayla's sudden altercation with the priest were a prophetic calling, preparing her for an ultimate and ghastly fate, what would follow came all too soon upon her tiny young body.

It wouldn't be long before she would find herself pinned down by the priest, shortly after being asked if she had hair in her private area. That question instigated by the priest was only the beginning of the nightmare that was about to ensue for little Shayla. Her attempt at an answer was not enough and her whimpering only emboldened her predator even more. This hapless nine-year-old girl was lost forever with no one to turn to—at a crossroads between her desperation for help and trying to be a good girl obeying her elders.

Flashbacks of the pornographic magazine Shayla had seen suddenly came flying forward, as she recalled seeing adults fucking, where she also saw their private hair as she attentively studied the shocking acts in the magazine.

She became more afraid, jolted from the recollection of the magazine pages, to suddenly facing her very present heinous priest. Back in his car, he pulled Shayla closer next to him while he drove. Just then, he took her little hand and placed it on top of his pants zipper. Shayla felt a noticeably big and hard thing in his pants that in her mind reminded her of the men's dicks she had seen in the porno magazine.

"Do you want to see it?" asked the priest while holding her towards him.

"I want to go home. My parents are waiting for me."

They arrived at the end of the dirt road where Shayla's house was, and before she had time to wonder if he was going to hold her back, he released her.

"Now, go on home and tell your parents you were a good girl. You know they always ask me if you were good. I will tell them again that you were a good girl. You do not want to make your father angry, do you? And you don't want your mother to be sad, do you?"

Shayla scooted over to the door, opened it and once again ran to her house as fast as she could without looking back to see if the priest's car was still there. She knew it was wrong for a man to want to touch a little girl. It didn't feel right. She also knew it was wrong for a man to force her hand on top of his private area.

Her father was the only man she had ever been near. He was a respectful man and would never touch his daughters in any way, like the priest. From that day forward, Shayla was afraid to go to choir practice.

They say life is not a magazine. No, sometimes the truth is stranger than fiction, with a harsh reality check not too far behind. The kind that robs from the young, the meek, and the innocent—leaving them numb and forever broken. *Still too young to process what was just taken away from them.*

Despite Shayla's best attempts to tell her mother she didn't want to go to choir practice anymore, her mother made her go, explaining it was good to give back to the church. They were poor and could not afford much. With Shayla being in the choir and participating in church activities, this was her parents' way of giving back to the church.

"But Mother, I don't like going."

"You must go, Shayla. It's good for you to go and I like when you sing in the church. You sound so beautiful and I am so proud of you."

"But Mother... I just don't like it and I don't really enjoy it."

"Your father is also very proud of you. He is so happy that you're being such a good girl."

"But Mother..."

"I don't want to talk about this anymore, Shayla! Your father wants you to be involved with the church and that's final! This is also a good way to keep you focused while having an activity to do. You don't want to disappoint your father, do you?"

The following week when choir practice had ended, Shayla contemplated walking home, but she quickly changed her mind when she realized it was dark. She was somewhat afraid of the dark.

She further considered that on her way home, there was a family with several watchdogs that were loose at nighttime. She had heard adults talking about those dogs being loose at night and how they would come out to the street and bark at anyone that got close to their property, and possibly also attack anyone walking by.

Shayla wanted to be the first one to be dropped off but knew the priest would never drop them off in that order, so she contemplated getting out of the car when any choir members were dropped off first. She would then walk home instead of waiting to be the last person dropped off.

This was her plan. However, it was past ten o'clock and as Shayla looked out the car window, she became reluctant to walk out of the car and walk or run away from the car. She knew the other passengers would definitely call her back or not allow her to walk home alone from any distant location. She then focused on a new plan where she would try to make it past the dogs.

Despite Shayla's best attempts to tell her mother she doesn't want to go to choir practice anymore, her mother makes her go as explaining it was good to give back to the church.

That evening was a perfect storm, literally, as it was pouring rain, making it a challenge to avoid the dogs. She would have to walk an extra thirty minutes just to get home. By that time, the priest would get there before her by car. She would have to muster all her inner-strength to run up the hill—with her sole aim of making it past the dogs. Either way, she knew she was in danger. *With the dogs or the priest!* The fear of being attacked by several watchdogs kept her inside the car, as she further realized that once everyone was dropped off, she would be alone in the car with the priest again. He would most definitely try to get her as he had before. Her throat began to tighten and she was not able to speak, as she anticipated what would follow next. Helpless, she just gazed out of the car window at the moon, staring blankly into the night as the time came when the last passenger would be dropped off.

Moment by moment, the terrifying threat of being alone with the priest intensified as she knew within minutes, he would ask her to move up to the front seat—further reminding that if she didn't comply, he would tell her father she was a bad girl.

The priest drove as fast as he could as if to show the last passengers he would get Shayla home as soon as possible. His driving haste was only a cover for his ulterior motive to stop, *and do the unthinkable.*

Once the car turned the corner, he slowed the vehicle down and as Shayla had feared, told her to move to the front seat.

She would often think that if there were no priests, then her life would be perfect and she could live perfectly happy. And free.

"Shayla, move up to the front seat! Do I have to warn you every time?"

"I'm just fine here. My parents are waiting for me. *I want to go home!"*

"Your father asked me if you were a good girl. So do your duty or else... If you don't move to the front seat, I will tell your father that you were not a good girl."

The priest suddenly reached over to the back seat and grabbed Shayla by her knee as she had wedged herself behind the passenger front seat. The priest then applied pressure to her knee, pulling her towards the middle as he stopped the vehicle, put it in park, turned around, and grabbed her with both hands.

"You must do your duty! You must be a good girl! You know what you have to do!"

The priest quickly hoisted the tiny Shayla to the front seat next to him. With his left hand, he unbuckled his pants and with his right arm around her, pulled her towards him where she was pressed tight against his big body. Her frame was so tiny that it was easy for him to maneuver his grip, as he reached his pants with his right hand and his left hand assisted with a quick tug pulling down his pants. He took Shayla's small hand in his and placed it around his erect cock, and had her stroke it.

With her eyes closed, she had suddenly escaped back to the

woods, collecting wildflowers to bring home to her mother. It was much easier to lose herself in imaginary thought, than it was to open her eyes to the monster before her and his vicious acts, where her tiny frame had been turned into a sexual instrument to his will and satisfaction.

Suddenly the priest let out an unrecognizable big yelp followed by a big sigh. Shayla opened her eyes and saw her hand all wet and slimy. The horrifying sight triggered another flashback when she had looked through the magazine and recalled seeing a white liquid in the pictures as people would lay with their eyes closed and mouths opened. She realized then that when people fuck, the white stuff is what was referred to as cum in the magazine.

Still holding on to Shayla's hand, the priest rubbed it inside his underwear as if to clean off his release, then pushed her away to the passenger seat towards the door.

"Now, that's a good girl. I will tell your father you're a good girl, Shayla."

Shayla did not say anything. She just opened the car door and ran home as fast as she could again. This time in the cold rain. When she got there, her mother and father were waiting for her.

"How was choir practice today, Shayla?" her mother asked.

"It was just fine, Mother."

"Did you learn any new songs?"

"No, Mother. No new songs. The same as last week."

The father further queried. "Were you a good girl, Shayla? You must remember to mind your manners. You do know that every time you go somewhere, you must always behave and do what the adults ask you to do. *Right?"*

"Yes, Father. I do everything that adults ask me to do. I am a good girl. Can I please go to bed now?"

"Yes, Shayla. You may go to bed. Don't forget to say your prayers."

"Yes, Father. I won't forget to say my prayers."

Shayla walked away from the kitchen into the dark bedroom where her sister was already asleep.

"Shayla, don't you want the light?" her father asked.

"No, Father. I don't need the light. I am not afraid of the dark anymore."

Shayla had always been afraid of the dark before and would never go into her bedroom without one of her parents carrying the kerosene light. Albeit on this horrific night, when everything had so severely changed for the young girl. *No light could ever be bright enough to blanket over the nightmare she had just experienced.*

Shayla's parents looked at each other with concern and worry.

"Did you notice something different about her?" prompted the mother.

"I did," acknowledged the father. "She didn't talk much to us and she also didn't stick around to listen to what we were talking about."

"I know and this is what I mean," said the mother.

"She also didn't wait for us to bring her to bed with the light," continued the father.

Her mother looked worried. She couldn't surmise what was wrong.

"Maybe she's just tired. We have to remember she is only a child doing more than most adults. She never stops," said the father, trying to calm down his wife. The thing was, the mother knew her daughter, and she was never tired. Instead, she realized it must be something else—something that was heavy on her mind.

The next day Shayla did not want to go outside. She lingered around her mother as if she wanted to say something, and was trying to find the right words.

Breaking the silence finally, her mother offered, "Shayla, would you like to learn how to play the mandolin so you can play it in church with the choir? It would be so great to see you play, and your father would be so proud of you."

"Mother, Father is always proud of me. He tells me everything... including how much of a good girl I am and how proud he is of me."

"Yes, Shayla. He is very proud of you. But imagine if you played an instrument? How even more proud he would be!"

"But Mother, I don't want to go to the choir anymore."

"Shayla, I have already talked to you about this. You cannot quit the choir, which you just started. *Remember?* It's good for you to go learn and keep yourself busy and focused. I think it would be great for you to learn how to play the mandolin. End of discussion."

"Yes, Mother," agreed Shayla reluctantly, gazing at the kitchen floor, trying to find the words and the courage to tell her mother the truth about the real reason why she didn't want to go to choir practice anymore.

Ignoring her daughter's plea, the mother later shared with her husband the idea of having Shayla learn how to play the mandolin. She explained to her husband that a girl like Shayla always had to learn something new, and this was something Shayla did well. Learn new things.

“We don't have the money to pay for her lessons," the father responded to his wife.

"I've been bringing fruits and vegetables to the parish house every week when I go sell after harvest. I never charge them and I'm sure our priest would never take the money anyway to simply teach a child of the parish how to play an instrument."

"You are right about that," acknowledged the father. “We are lucky to have a priest like him. We all know there is nothing that man wouldn't do for anyone in this village."

The following Sunday after church, Shayla's parents stayed behind in the hopes of talking to the priest.

"Hello Father, how are you?" Shayla's father started the conversation.

"Doing well, sir. How's everything?" asked the priest with a slight tinge of nervous tension in his voice. He couldn't tell where the parents' conversation was going, or where it was coming from. And if Shayla had said anything to them about the other night in his car.

“Shayla has been doing great singing in the choir," offered the priest in his attempt to steer the chat. “She's a smart little girl."

"Thank you, Father. Indeed, we are quite proud of her and actually would like to ask if you might consider teaching her how to play the mandolin? My wife and I both feel it would be beneficial for Shayla to learn something new, as she has a lot of energy and is so active. She really loves to learn new things."

"Absolutely!" the maniacal priest blurted without hesitation. "I would most definitely be happy to teach her. She's so smart, it won't take much time. I trust she will pick up the mandolin quite quickly."

"Great, when can she start?" Shayla's mother asked.

"She can start tomorrow. Have her come to the church right after school."

"We don't have money to pay you, but we can supply you and your mother with whatever you need from the farm," proposed Shayla's father in a humbled voice.

"Don't be silly, sir. You do more than most people. No need to pay me money at all. I would be glad to help with Shayla's lessons, compliments of the church."

The priest glanced over at a nervous Shayla, who was standing there the whole time as her parents chatted with him. With a forced smile and a borderline evil glint in his eyes, the priest extended his hand to the oblivious father as a show of support that he could rely on him to teach Shayla her music lessons.

The mandolin is a fifteen-string musical instrument that some people in the choir would play. Because Shayla was part of the choir, her parents believed she was smart enough and would learn to play it quickly. It was their dream to see her play an instrument while attending church. However, under the guise of the music lessons with the revered village priest, the parents remained unaware of Shayla's dread toward him. Instead, they continued to put their faith in the priest to teach their little girl. Had they only known the truth, *but they didn't.*

So when it was time to go for her mandolin practice, Shayla would hide in the woods in the hopes of not being found. There she would wait anxiously in silence for long periods, allowing the time of her lessons to pass. From her safe hiding place, she could see the only afternoon bus of the day go by, from which she would gauge the perfect time to go home. Then one day she fell asleep in the woods while waiting to see the bus go by and did not wake up until dusk.

When she got home, the priest was there because her parents had alerted him that Shayla had never come home. The priest was showing his concern for Shayla's disappearance while her parents grew increasingly worried once they found out Shayla never showed up for any of her music lessons. Her parents demanded that she tell them where she had been, but Shayla did not talk. Her throat tightened and no words came out. Her parents were embarrassed, apologizing to the priest for their daughter's actions. They assured the priest Shayla would be going to her music lesson the following day and she would also be sent to confession at church the following Sunday before services.

When the priest left their house that day, Shayla's parents sat her down and asked her where she had been going all those days instead of going to her music lessons.

Shayla could not talk about it to her parents because she didn't want her father to think she was not a good girl. After many unsuccessful attempts to find out where Shayla had been going, her parents dismissed her and she went to bed.

What would soon follow, next to Shayla's inevitable *pseudo* music lessons, was the priest having his ways, and repeatedly, with the little girl.

Her earlier childhood as "happy," that purity and innocence, had ceased to exist. What would follow were more violent rapes by the priest—leaving Shayla to wipe her bloody tears from her latest attack. Her tiny body could only do so much, and didn't have the strength, to fend off her offender. Despite her internal cries for help, that no one heard or came to her rescue, she remained resilient in her silence for fear of shame.

Young Shayla didn't want to be judged and was more keen on simply pleasing her parents, at all costs, including to her physical and emotional welfare. She continued to wallow in shame. Besieged by these vile attacks made Shayla suicidal, blaming herself for what happened. She would often wonder, *what kind of man would take advantage of a poor little girl like this?* And of all people, the esteemed priest of the village church. Did lust and greed take over his mind and lead him to such brutal acts?

Shayla would bathe herself frequently, as she tried to remove any residual stench of the priest from herself—the dirty old man who left her with nightmares of his foul and overpowering body on top of hers. *What had she done to deserve such a horrifying experience? What had this world become?*

The damage from this incessant experience at the contemptible hands of the priest fueled Shayla's feelings of inadequacy. It became hard to look at herself. *She didn't think she was good enough, beautiful or pretty enough, hating everything about her appearance, as she stopped recognizing herself in the mirror.*

She felt tremendous shame which muted any attempt to tell her parents, for fear they would not understand. For all her attempts to escape the priest, she had become his sex slave. To be so young and contemplating her end-all exit...

CHAPTER 6

Open Road Trip

Present Day.

It had been a long day for Emma with back-to-back client appointments and barely time to breathe in between. She was still beaming from all the excitement of her recent reunion with her dear old friend, Juliette. She was further grateful to their mutual acquaintance, Mary, for reconnecting them. Emma couldn't wait to rush home and start preparing for her planned road trip with Juliette that would start the following morning. It was all set. A three-day excursion between the two women on a comfortable, leisurely journey along the open road. This was their chance to share about what happened with the wretched priest before each woman left the island forever. Emma wanted no distractions coming between her anticipated heart-to-heart exchange with Juliette.

Exhausted when she got home, Emma made a straight b-line to her bathroom and started to run a bath. She really needed to decompress in the comfort of her soaker tub. While the water filled, she poured in some suds, then went to her phone to turn on her favorite Pandora channel, as the Helen Reddy classic, "I Am Woman," came on...

I am woman, hear me roar...

With the music playing in the background, Emma returned to her bath and lit some candles. Pulling off her clothes she stepped in and laid in the bubbly bath. The water felt warm and soothing. Taking in a deep sigh of relief from the day, she closed her eyes and surrendered to this welcome moment. In an imaginary state, she started to role-play the events of her road trip with Juliette. *How would it go?* After all, their planned trip would be starting the following morning—a day Emma had been looking forward to since first inviting Juliette.

There was so much she wanted to say to Juliette. *But how would she start? What would be the right opening statement to break the ice along the road? How would Juliette react? Would Juliette share with Emma as well?* Before a next thought could enter her mind, she had fallen into a momentary lapse surrounded in all the bubbles. She quickly opened her eyes and completed her bath.

Without knowing more about Emma's intentions, though she had a feeling, Juliette looked forward to joining her on the road. Several years older than Emma, she believed her past on the island with the priest had become a long-buried secret. In fact, since her departure from her homeland, she had almost forgotten herself—making it a lifelong effort to never think about it. And for the longest time, that seemed to work. Until Emma invited her on the road trip. Juliette anticipated the reason was far greater than just a casual visit with an old friend.

She flashed on memories of the predatory priest and how rumors had circulated in their village that she was his mistress. When she decided to leave her island home, she was afraid the priest would find a new girl to replace her. Protective of a much younger Shayla at the time, she had suspected she could become his next prey and tried to warn her the day of her departure. *Did the priest force himself on Emma as well?* Juliette pondered though she couldn't tell, nor could she pick up any cues from her at Mary's dinner where they had reconnected.

All these years later, and soon about to join her old friend for a long drive, Juliette became more anxious and prepared for a potentially tough conversation. Though she tried to stay positive and not overthink the forbidden topic.

As Juliette was about to discover, their new journey would open up so much between the women and be a path toward healing. A safe space of sharing and letting go.

At the same time, all Emma wanted was for the two women to lose themselves in each other's trust. To reveal their own experiences with the priest. As horrifying as it was, the women needed to talk about it. And if it took a whole weekend getaway for the women to open up and dig deep into their own truths about what happened to them, then so be it. Emma was just fine with making their destination unknown and winging their time on the road.

When the next morning came, Emma was ready for it. She woke early. The sound of that first wake-up bell was a welcome reminder that her planned road trip with Juliette was finally here. This would be the first day. She jumped out of bed and started to get ready. Juliette would be arriving in the next hour. Just then, the phone rang and Emma's heart sank as she noticed it was Juliette calling. She desperately hoped it was not to cancel. Emma reluctantly picked up the phone.

"Hello," she answered nervously.

"Hey Emma," a nimble Juliette chimed with no hint of changing plans. "So, I'm about to load up my car for our drive and wondered if I should bring anything, besides a change of clothes?"

"Hey Juliette, just bring your wonderful self," replied Emma with a big sigh of relief. "I've got everything else. We'll let the open road be our guide on this new adventure. I'm thrilled to see where it takes us."

"Sounds like a perfect plan. Works for me! See you shortly."

"See you!"

The women hung up and Emma tried to get a grip, aligning the emotions she was trying to contain during her call with Juliette.

An hour later, Juliette arrived and sent a quick text to Emma. She waited in her car for her to come down. In a flurry, having just responded to Juliette, Emma grabbed her things in one-fell swoop and flew out her door. Juliette jumped out of her car when she saw Emma trying to power through her building entry with all her things.

> **Protective of a much younger Shayla at the time, she had suspected she could become his next prey and tried to warn her the day of her departure.**

Juliette was older than Emma by more than ten years. A beautiful woman with dark curls, she exuded an air of hard-earned wisdom and strength. “Here, let me help you,” she offered as she met Emma at the top of her stairs. She grabbed one of her bags.

They headed down the stairs together and Juliette followed Emma to her car where they threw everything in the back seat. They smiled and gave each other a long hug—a hug that felt like they were making up for the lost years between them.

“I’m going to grab my stuff,” said Juliette as she broke free to run to her car.

She returned to Emma’s car and they took off. It was a beautiful sunny day, like a prophetic glow lighting up the course of the day. Emma entered an adjoining highway off the main road and turned on the radio. Music came on and filled her car. After a few miles of just sitting quietly without a spoken word between them, Emma tried to speak above the music.

“So,” she said, stretching her voice as the music was overpowering her attempt. Before trying to speak again, she abruptly turned off the radio.

“Hope you don’t mind,” she said apologetically to Juliette. “Of course, it would be much easier to chat without the music. I don’t know what I was thinking when I turned on the radio.”

“That’s perfectly fine,” Juliette comforted. “I am just so glad that we are doing this… finally getting together and catching up after all these years. This visit has been long overdue. I mean, what were the odds that we would both know Mary and reconnect like this? This is absolutely incredible and a real blessing for us both."

"Yes, no kidding," Emma continued. "There is so much I need to say. I really don't know where the best place to start is, but here we go..." Taking a deep breath, "Do you remember when the priest offered music lessons to the children in our old village?"

"I do remember," replied Juliette, sounding a bit apprehensive, knowing where their chat was headed and too close to her own personal experience with the priest. Though she wanted Emma to start it. *The anticipated heart-to-heart talk.* "Yes my dear and I'm afraid I already know where you are going with this. But please go on."

Taking her lead from Juliette, Emma continued, "Well, you may remember I was just a young girl back then, still a child only around nine, and I was among his music students. And dare I say, unfortunately this is the time when my nightmare began with this very bad and evil man, our village priest."

With a pause, she took a deep breath. "What he did to me continues to haunt me to this day."

As the car made its way up the road, Emma's voice faded into a surreal vacuum—with her words transcended into inaudible moving lips. Juliette had suddenly lapsed into a momentary flashback. The priest suddenly appeared on top of her. In her youth and brutalized, she tried to fight him off but had lost her battle and the remaining soul of her one-time innocence.

"Juliette, are you okay?" Emma prompted, noticing her friend seemed somewhere else.

The motionless Juliette shuddered as Emma's voice resumed its volume. She broke her silence, "I'm sorry this happened to you, *too,* but you are not alone here, Emma. Or may I call you as I remember? *Shayla?"*

Emma was leveled by Juliette's words, especially hearing her real name again. Not sure how to respond, she uttered a reluctant, "Sure." She knew it was safe to let her guard down with Juliette. It was time to confront her demons and trust her friend to help her find that courage.

Despite their heavy topic to start, the women also reminisced about the better days back on the island. While Emma and Juliette's reunion was a long time coming and held tremendous significance for the two victims sharing a common secret, Emma was not prepared for all the feelings that would be conjured up. She always knew she had to talk to someone and that someone couldn't have been more perfect than Juliette—her long lost friend from her homeland that she could relate to.

The two were inextricably tied together. She knew Juliette would understand and commiserate between their shared past and pain. Juliette had gone through the same horrifying experience with the priest—someone like Emma who had endured the trauma and vile attacks of their treacherous priest.

This trip meant an opportunity for healing. A time of compassion and closure for the women.

Next to their unfortunate shared experience, Emma believed there also had to be others. Her heart sank feeling a pain so deeply ingrained. Not just for herself, but feeling incensed to what other helpless victims could have also gone through, like she and Juliette had with the priest. She was sick to her stomach. Just then, Emma veered off the shoulder of the road and suddenly slammed on the breaks. She opened her door and ran out into a bush to vomit. Then returned to the car.

"Are you okay?" Juliette was concerned about her friend as she reached into her bag to grab a bottle of water. She handed it to Emma who drank without saying a word. Then broke her silence.

"Thank you, Juliette. I am so terribly sorry about this. I really don't want to create any discomfort here. It's been such a long hard road for me in all these years since we last saw each other back home, as I can certainly imagine it's been for you as well.

"I just knew there was something off about you when we said our goodbyes then and you were all packed up to go. I remember that moment of seeing you for the last time so vividly. It was as if you couldn't wait to leave. I was too young then and really didn't understand your haste. Until now. Of course, having gone through it myself, with the priest as well, *and the reason for leaving,* I totally understand in more intimate ways than I care to think about anymore. It makes me shudder. I was much younger and there was really no way for me to know that I would be his next victim...

"Until after you left and my parents made me take his music lessons. That's when my world and youth, as I remembered it, radically shifted and turned upside down, *fast.* I was violated by this beast and repeatedly. This went on even as I continued to grow into my tenth and eleventh years of age. I was still too young for any of this to happen, but it did. *To me and to you.* I hate him for what he did to us.

"If I had the strength and the courage back then, I would have killed him. But I didn't. Instead, I just decided to leave the island for good, like you. Everything about it reminded me of my real-life nightmare with this vile priest. And that's just it. Even when I don't think about what he did to me, those feelings still consume my soul. But now hearing about your direct and unfortunate experience with this sick man, it seems like you had it worse over a longer period. I am sorry for that. For you to have endured such vicious assaults. It makes me sick. *Absolutely sick!* And here we are again. I can't stand it! What it did to us both."

This was the first time ever that Emma had shared her story with anyone. Though she knew Juliette was the absolute right one to open up to—her wise, older long-lost soul sister. Reunited again.

"You poor, poor girl," consoled Juliette. "It sounds like he threatened you the same way he had threatened me. I was also too young then to better understand why this was happening to me. I just knew what he did was so wrong, but he also scared me into feeling like I had no other choice than to comply to his will. I literally became his sex slave. *I spit on his grave!* Now hearing your story, I better understand how after I left it was like he made you my replacement, you poor dear. I am so terribly sorry this even happened to you.

"No young girl should ever experience such vulgar acts from an adult man. And in our unfortunate case, this was not just a man, he was our village priest. Our people worshipped him. He could do no wrong in their eyes. But remove the veil and this was what this monster was truly all about."

Hearing Juliette's words comforted Emma. She had so wanted to be done with her pain and shame held to for too long. She was ready to turn over a new and vibrant chapter in her life, for good. She had to. Her future depended on it. Juliette was a way forward for her—a threshold to the other side of releasing what haunted her for years and a new chance to heal.

> **"But now hearing about your direct and unfortunate experience with this sick man, it seems like you had it worse over a longer period."**

As their road trip ensued, harnessed between the greenery of the woods, Emma shared with Juliette her desire to publicly tell her story someday as part of her effort to set herself free. Alternatively, Juliette was more reticent about this topic altogether and tried not to engage further. "I would rather die with the details of my time on the island than to publicly shame myself." She continued, "But I want you to know that I appreciate hearing your story. I really appreciate that you shared it with me, which has already made a world of difference. You see, for many years I also felt the need to speak up, though I could never really muster the courage to come forward and open up to anyone."

"I completely understand Juliette," offered a consoling Emma. "You have my word that I would never reveal to anyone the details of your abuse with the pedophile priest. If the locals only knew, including our very own parents, but would they have believed us?"

How could they get past all the hurt the priest had caused them? There was no justice for them. He had threatened them to remain silent. And it worked. They were. Silent. Crying only on the inside, where no one could hear them. Now everyone they could talk to were gone. The parents. The priest. And the tight-knit villagers who were like an extended family to the women during their youth.

In the course of their chat, the old friends realized there had to be other girls back on the island who had gone through the same dreadful experience with the priest. Emma and Juliette couldn't be the only ones singled out by him. There had to be more who were molested and raped by this predator. An investigation had to be done. Though he had been long deceased, the women contemplated and committed to some kind of justice for his actions. *But what? And how?*

As their first day on the road wore into night, they checked into a motel along the way. After only one day, the two women had created a tight bond and a new lifetime of memories that Emma would never forget.

In the motel, as Juliette was preparing to go to bed, she appeared quite frail. Something was off with her energy. Later that night, Emma wandered the grounds of the motel. In her stroll, she encountered a family coming out of the diner downstairs. They were a stark reminder to her of what a family looked like; something she had missed since leaving the island. She tried to avoid any contact, but the young girl with the family broke away—another reminder to Emma of her perky streak as a child, before the priest broke her spirit. She caught the little girl before she got too far from her family.

The mother was grateful. "Thank you. I'm afraid she's had too much sugar."

Before Emma could answer, a siren was heard getting closer to the motel. It suddenly stopped. She was startled and ran toward the flashing lights of an ambulance that had parked in front of the stairway to her room. As she looked up adjacent to the top of the stairs, she saw some commotion coming from inside her room. Just then she also saw the front desk manager stepping out of their room who was walking behind two paramedics carrying a gurney with a body. Emma panicked, realizing that it must have been Juliette, though she didn't understand what could have happened in the brief time since she left their room.

The men made their way down, practically bumping into Emma who was standing at the foot of the stairs in a state of shock. She quickly moved out of everyone's way while also tending to her friend who appeared lifeless on the gurney. She reached for

Juliette's hand. Utterly dazed, she was trying to process this unforeseen event.

"What happened?" Emma shouted at the manager who was still walking behind the paramedics.

"Sorry ma'am," the paramedic started. "Your friend was found unconscious by the room door. It appears she fell right outside the door and hit her head badly on the metal railing."

Desperate to be there for her friend, Emma turned to one of the men, "I'm her friend. I need to come with her."

The manager motioned to the paramedics, acknowledging she was telling the truth.

Emma felt faint. *How could this freak accident happen?* She had only been gone from their room for a few minutes.

"Let me grab my purse," she shouted back, running upstairs to the room she had shared with Juliette for just a short while. She found her purse and also grabbed Juliette's purse in case she needed to find a close contact to reach. Closing the door behind her, she ran down to meet everyone in the ambulance.

They helped her to hop in as she went to sit by Juliette's side, reaching for her hand again. Emma's face was covered in a pool of tears. They took off as the siren sounded off.

"Wake up, Juliette. Wake up! Can you hear me? I am here. It's me. *Shayla.*" Juliette did not respond.

"Ma'am, she is unconscious," said a paramedic. "I'm sorry but she can't hear you now."

The small EKG monitoring machine hanging overhead suddenly started to ding as its display shifted from a jagged perpendicular movement to a flat-line reading. *The incredible seemed to be happening right before Emma's eyes.*

It was the next morning. Emma was walking out of a hospital. She was alone and appeared completely exhausted and disoriented. A cab was waiting by the main entry and she hopped in. Nothing could have prepared her for the unforeseen events of the previous night with her friend. Juliette didn't make it.

The two women had made an incredible connection during their suddenly preempted road trip. They created an intimate and unbreakable bond, though now in spirit. They had talked about many things which altogether made a profound impact on Emma and helped her reach a place of forgiveness. To be free and release her shame from the past. It was time to move forward. *To move on.* She knew Juliette would have wanted it that way.

The heartbroken Emma remained in grief for days. Juliette had become her best friend for what seemed too short a time. She had learned so much during their reconnected, albeit brief, span together and desperately wanted to hold on to every precious moment of their shared intimacy.

Though Juliette had floated in and out of consciousness at the hospital, Emma would never forget the look on her friend's face as she closed her eyes in her arms for the last time. Juliette was the definition of a true friend, thicker than blood. Emma had confided so much in her before she would take her last breath. They shared it *all* with each other—the bad and the worst of times with the priest.

Juliette's death was a wakeup call and a reminder that life was too short. It's not promised to anyone, next to the events in one's life. Emma had discovered the hard way that just because she was only nine at the time, it didn't mean she was untouchable. She wasn't safe—even inside her own circle of trust, with her parents, who had pressed the music lessons on her with the priest.

Since her trip with Juliette, Emma was able to make peace with her mother before she passed away. She also forgave the priest for what he had done to her. *An emotional bridge she needed to cross to be truly free.* She knew reaching this place of forgiveness was her only way to true healing and to becoming a stronger version of herself.

One evening after work, Emma went home and pulled out her stationary. *She started to write and write...*

CHAPTER 7

The Attack

Fifty years in the past.

When children rely on their parents for protection, and parents in turn rely on their community leaders and clergy for support and guidance, that circle of trust is how families thrive and what societies are built on—a tight-knit fabric that starts at home where the heart is. However, there is no telling when the lines are blurred and the leaders, who represent support for families, are actually predators who prey on their followers, and their children. The weak, the vulnerable, and the unaware—of their otherwise guise—concealing their true evil nature and intent. So was the instance when the village priest, had requested specifically for Shayla's help with his mother over the following summer. Her father, who looked up to the priest, appreciated his gesture toward his daughter. However, she knew all too well the priest's ulterior motives and was terrified at the thought of what would lie ahead. A fate from which there would be no return.

With no way around her parents' insistence that she continue her music lessons with the priest, Shayla, in her best effort to be a good girl, did as she was told. *As if intuiting the tragic events that loomed ahead—a feeling of dread she could not shake ate at her insides.*

Before the attacks had started in the priest's home, Shayla was initially molested at the church hall where the choir would go to practice. As her music lessons would evolve in the priest's home, she arrived begrudgingly from the safety and comfort of her home.

There, the priest's attacks would escalate and the most vile sexual acts were committed and repeatedly—with nowhere to escape for young Shayla, then only ten years old.

As Shayla would continue to show up for her weekly lessons at the priest's home, the attacks became worse and more violent. As time passed, she considered her stolen innocence at the reprehensible hands of the priest. Like a pendulum swaying from side-to-side, she thought of suicide, but then dreamt of killing the priest. She was so disgusted by him, it made her feel ill.

Most days she would vomit from a mix of emotions, wavering between feeling suicidal, to suddenly so vengeful and fierce—where she couldn't sleep until her mission to kill the priest was completed. *And she had to be the one behind the act to kill.* She had to see his blood on her hands and had determined it was her only way toward true peace. The more she thought about it, the more she was fixed on her plan to kill the evil pedophile priest.

What began as a music lesson making progress, normal at first, however it devolved quickly into molestation—as Shayla was forced to perform oral sex on the priest. Though not quite a full rape at this early stage of the priest's mock music lessons, this would later happen in the following summer after she was forced to go live at his house for the season, under the further guise of helping his mother with her chores.

On the first day of summer vacation, the priest made an unexpected visit to Shayla's house and asked to speak to her father in private. The two of them engaged in deep conversation and appeared to be talking about her as they kept veering their attention to her across the room. The priest had meticulously planned his visit to her house—not wanting to alarm her of his arrival and to make it a surprise, albeit an unwelcome one.

The priest had carefully picked his timing and well-crafted words with her father. He had to appear convincing, overshadowing the actual intent and malice behind his visit. His sudden arrival hit Shayla hard as if she was thrown off a cliff; falling into an abyss of horror where she knew her nightmare with the priest would only get worse.

At first there was no sign of Shayla when the priest first came to her house. He was disappointed but took the opportunity to speak with her father, alone, so she would not have time to plan an escape. What the priest was not aware of was that Shayla had heard a car come up the dirt road and from her backyard was able to see it was the priest. She hid behind the shed and was able to hear their whole conversation.

"How are you?" The father welcomed, nescient and always happy to see the priest. "What can I do for you, sir?"

The priest greeted Shayla's father with a handshake and started his ploy. "Well, as you know, my mother is elderly now and I'm quite busy at the church. She requested if you and your wife would allow Shayla to spend the summer with her and keep her company."

"Of course," responded Shayla's father without hesitancy. "Whatever you and your mother need, and if we can help, we will."

Shortly after the conversation between the two men, Shayla's father called her. "Go pack some clothes, Shayla," he ordered. "You are going to the priest's parish house this summer to help his mother."

Shayla's father spoke with such authority, there was no pleading with him otherwise. Their dynamic was quite clear and decisive. When he spoke, Shayla did as told.

"Do as he and his mother say," the father continued. "Don't be an embarrassment to me!"

The father thought of his words, adding, "You're a special and smart girl, Shayla. The priest's mother has requested *you* to help her during school vacation, and this is a good opportunity for you, girl. And you won't have to help me on the farm."

Shayla's dark curls covered her face, suddenly sullen and seriously concerned that her life was in jeopardy. She wore a cute little dress the local seamstress lady had made for her and wore no shoes fresh from playing out in the yard.

Feeling completely defeated and shattered by her father's announcement, she looked up at him with her dried soft pink lips in a big panic, perplexed, with a cautionary look—as if hoping he could read her frightened face, *"Don't make me do this!"*

Desperate she started her plea, saying the first thing that came to mind, "But Father, I promised Mother I'd help her this summer." She kept looking at him, anxious for him to see the fear in her face, hoping to alarm him to not to go forward with the plan to the priest's home. Despite her throwing an even deeper worried look at her father, he remained oblivious and firm in his command of his daughter.

Fresh from his arrival, the priest was still standing there with Shayla's father during her failed attempted appeal. He nonchalantly smoked a cigarette as he kept looking at her, reveling in her fright. He enjoyed watching her in this moment of dread, helpless to defy her father. She was afraid to leave but had no choice. In a frozen state, she headed to her small bedroom in the back of the house and abided to her father's orders. As she gathered some clothes, she kept thinking about how he could be so blind and senseless to the blatant signs of fear on her face. She knew once behind the closed doors of the priest's home, she was doomed and there was nothing she could do about it. It would be the worst nightmare from which there would be no turning back from. Her chest suddenly tightened as she also felt a piercing bellyache and dizziness. She could not shake the sense that something horribly wrong was about to happen.

Consumed with unimaginable fright, she panicked over thoughts of being alone with the priest. Just then, she heard her father call out her name again.

"Shayla, hurry up! You should never make anyone wait for you!" Yelling from the kitchen door, her father waited for a response.

"Coming!" Shayla shouted back. She quickly threw her clothes into a bag and looked for her tiny flip-flops under the edge of her bed before walking out onto the patio where the priest stood with his cigarette hanging from the side of his mouth. Once they were out of the house, the priest threw the cigarette on the ground, stomping on it with the tip of his shoe.

With a look of triumph and practically gloating, he walked slowly towards his car and snapped his finger at Shayla, motioning for her to get in the car when her father wasn't looking. She sat in the back seat like she had many times before in her attempt to keep a distance from her predator. She was horrified and couldn't breathe as she sensed the priest was certain to touch her and possibly lay on her.

Shayla's mother always taught her to never, ever allow anyone to touch her private parts or to expose herself to anyone regardless of whom. Her mother had also told her how babies are made, and that only married women should have babies. Even though Shayla was only ten years old at this time, she already knew a lot about being an adult. After she had seen earlier in the magazine about having sex, she would take any opportunity to listen to adults to see if she might learn more about it. She always pretended to be playing and not paying attention when adults were talking, but she was quite curious and she always listened to as many adult gossipy conversations as she could when she had the chance. Her mother tried to teach her to mind her business and not ask questions to adults. However, young Shayla had a knack for positioning herself in such a way that she could still hear everything.

The mere thought of the priest sticking his hard cock in her frightened Shayla so much that she knew her life was in danger.

Her solution and ultimate plan was to kill the priest—something that needed to be put into action fast, as her greatest fear was about to happen.

Back at the priest's house in the patio area, the priest had cornered Shayla as he suddenly grabbed her small, tender, newly developed breasts and squeezed them. Then without warning he suddenly punched her with all his force. As he suspected, she did not cry or make any sound.

"Cry cockroach, cry!" he demanded.

"No, I will never cry for you," said Shayla, looking at him as if she could kill him right then. "I will never, never, cry for you. You disgust me! I hate you and I will kill you!"

She knew once behind the closed doors of the priest's home, she was doomed and there was nothing she could do about it.

He reached down to the ground, and he picked her up with his left hand and he slapped her across the face again with his right hand. The slap to the face pushed her against the stone wall forcefully and she fell to the ground again.

An expression of terror came over Shayla, as she closed her eyes, trying to escape in her head—the inescapable, her predator. Her arms felt limp beside her small body. She was lightheaded, and at that very moment, Shayla believed she was having an encounter with death. She didn't feel any strength or desire to keep up the fight. Numbness had riddled her body. It was over. He had won.

All of a sudden, Shayla opened her eyes and realized she was not dead. She felt no pain at all. She got up and just as she had a plan to run around him, he grabbed her by the bottom end of her dress and pulled her towards him.

She pulled away, but he pulled her so forcefully towards him that the dress ripped and a piece of it tore off her body. He stood there with a piece of the ripped child's dress in his hand and a cigarette hanging from the side of his mouth. Shayla had ducked to the ground when her dress got ripped off her body, and quickly crawled over to the stone wall in the patio.

She bent her knees with both of her hands wrapped around to cover the front of her body. She then swung her head in such a way so her long curly hair could cover the front of her upper body where her small breasts would not be exposed.

Her childish vulnerability was thrilling to the priest. It was much more exciting than he expected as he regaled in her defenselessness, despite her resistance. He lit another cigarette and just grinned at her, emboldened by her fear.

"Remember all those times that you got away?" he started. "All those times that you didn't show up for your music lesson? You should have been a good girl and done what you were asked."

"You're an evil and bad man, and I will never be your good girl!" Shayla retaliated. "I'm just a child. Be a good man, *Padre,* and let me be!"

He moved closer toward her, aiming to slap her, but she ducked as she quickly spread and bore her tiny frame along the ground. She did not say another word as she anticipated the worst was about to happen to her from the man she totally loathed.

Shamed and in agony, with nowhere to run, her weakness excited him even more. He dropped the piece of torn dress he was holding, and grabbed Shayla this time by her hair—picking her off the ground like a dead weight as she hardly stood on her own. He let go of her hair, but quickly grabbed her by the arm and spun her around to the middle of the patio area where there was an old stone table.

Shayla's physical state became even more frozen as her small body suddenly went into shock and started to tremble out of control. Just then she could smell the soft sweet scent of the concord grapes hanging from the vine. She opened her eyes and saw the vine bearing fruit.

In her effort to drift from the pain, she imagined tasting the grapes. She further imagined the grapes bursting in her mouth as she smelled the soft scent. Going deeper with her imagination, she next saw herself running through a vineyard, with a view of the ocean from her father's farm, where she could also hear his affectionate voice.

"Shayla, make sure you don't step on the grapes," he would caution.

for a new cigarette. He lit the cigarette and walked away.

While Shayla's father remained unaware of what was truly happening at the priest's mother's house—the violent and horrific rape attack on his daughter—he just sat at home, consumed with the greatest pride for his daughter being a *good girl,* and how she would soon be the best mandolin player in the village.

However, it was quite an alternate universe for young Shayla, back at the priests, where the real-life nightmare she had suffered had caused her to lapse in and out of consciousness. Despite this tragic event, her fear of shame was far greater, as she wallowed to herself, remaining resilient in her silence.

There was a dark dim light above the door in the patio in the back of the house. After a brief state of shock and bewilderment from the attack, when Shayla looked up, she saw a door open and to her surprise, it was the priest's elderly mother. She had watched everything from behind the curtains, unmoved, and only observant from a distance.

Once the rape was over, she went outside to Shayla's aid. She was holding a sheet and put it over her, helping Shayla off the stone patio table. The mother guided her inside. Still leveled by the attack, Shayla stumbled a few times as the priest's mother helped her every time to regain her footing. Once inside, the mother handed a wet towel to Shayla to clean herself. She cared for her injuries.

In that brief moment, the priest's mother attempted some words of solace, "I know your pain." Though Shayla knew all too well the mother could never imagine her pain.

While his mother didn't condone her son's acts, she kept mum as if she feared him—right down to that ghastly night of terror when she witnessed a frail young Shayla getting violently raped, physically ripped apart, in her own home. She saw everything and yet said nothing. *Was Shayla not the only one he had threatened in the mother's house?*

> **While Shayla's father remained unaware of what was truly happening at the priest's mother's house—the violent and horrific rape attack on his daughter—he just sat at home, consumed with the greatest pride for his daughter being a good girl.**

Shayla dealt with insurmountable pain from her injuries. Though she had suspected he would try to touch her, her big rape was so incredibly violent, she was not prepared for his vicious actions on her small body, as he appeared even more monstrous in size next to her. The nightmare with the evil priest had only just begun that summer. Following the attack, Shayla could not wait to bathe herself to remove his stench on her.

Later that night the mother encouraged Shayla to go to sleep but the violated young girl was still too enraged from what her son had done to her. Instead, she laid awake as a flood of tears poured from her eyes. She could not believe what had just happened to her. That she was violated by the most horrid and unimaginable of acts at her young age of ten. Her mind ran wild with a flurry of concerns: *Why would the priest rape a child? Why would he do this to me? What have I done to deserve this? I am just an innocent little girl who wanted to please her parents. My parents would be horrified if they knew this happened to me. I don't know what to do or where to go. I am in the middle of nowhere. I have no one to help me. I have no one that I can trust. I am only thankful for his mother, though I don't believe she is to be really trusted. Why would he choose me to be his helpless victim? I want to go home. I don't want to be here anymore. I have cried so much to relieve my pain, but it does not make me feel better. The only thing that will make me feel better is killing this man, but I need a plan.*

The more Shayla thought about what the priest had done to her, so did her thoughts intensify of killing him. She knew if she took a knife and snuck into his room while he was sleeping, she could stick the knife in his neck and he would bleed to death.

Then when his mother would find him dead the next morning, Shayla would pretend she was sleeping. She would not be still until she could get her revenge. She was determined to kill him at any cost.

When Shayla finally fell asleep after the attack, she experienced a lucid dream where the priest had disappeared from her life and from his mother. While there was no sign of him around, Shayla feared he would return.

The stress of the priest weighed on her so heavily, it gnawed at her swollen throat with such pain, it felt as if she could choke and could not speak. She went back to thoughts of killing the priest as her body remained still. She then opened her eyes and looked up at the ceiling, but wasn't sure if the pain she was feeling was real or if it was a really bad dream.

She was tired of hurting in silence, and decided she could wait no longer to kill her predator.

Even in a dream state, her shattered soul knew the violent attack she had survived was real. She wished it was all just a bad dream she could wake up from, though the pain wouldn't lose its grasp. Falling into a deeper sleep, she was caught between the blur of her conscious and unconscious state—as she contemplated more ways to kill the evil priest. In her dream, she finally got the courage to kill him.

She got up from her bed and silently went into the kitchen looking for the right knife to kill him in his sleep. As she walked to the kitchen, she looked around to see if anyone was awake, but all were sleeping. The house was pitch black, so she took her time getting there, cautiously trying not to set off any unexpected sounds. When she finally made it to the kitchen, there was no silverware on the table to be found. She then opened the kitchen drawer slowly and looked around. To her surprise there was one knife and she took it.

With her heart pounding, she walked slowly to the priest's room. Beads of sweat gave way to her movement in the shadows of the darkness. She didn't realize the knife was slowly sliding out of her hand until it landed on the floor. When she picked it up, she grabbed the wrong angle of the knife and cut herself with its sharp edge.

Just then she heard someone coming and she ran into the hallway closet as her blood dripped across the floor. To her astonishment, it was the priest. He turned on all the lights and looked around to see where the noise came from. Shayla's heart raced frantically as she heard his footsteps approaching. The priest followed the trail of blood on the floor, leading him to the closet door. He opened it and suddenly Shayla lunged at him with all her might, stabbing him in his belly as the knife went deep into his body. The priest gasped in shock and tried to fight back but couldn't breathe. He fell to the floor as he cried out for help.

Shayla was standing over his body, gleaming with satisfaction, and relief in her eyes. She finally got the revenge she wanted. Though little did she realize the priest's mother was standing behind her and ready to kill Shayla.

How could this be happening? The young girl wondered as everything was moving fast.

"Turn around slowly Shayla and put your hands up," the mother commanded in an eerie tone. "You are not a good girl."

Shayla was surprised to see the priest's mother suddenly there with an old shotgun pointed at her. It was the same gun displayed above the kitchen door, occasionally used to scare neighborhood dogs off the property. Shayla attempted to speak with some form of apology, but the mother was stern and motioned for the girl to be still. She didn't want to hear anything from Shayla.

At that moment without warning, the mother pulled the trigger and shot Shayla who collapsed to the floor.

"Father, please forgive me," the girl uttered her last words as she touched her wounded chest in disbelief.

Just as she closed her eyes, Shayla quickly opened them and

looked around before realizing it was all a dream. She instantly woke up from her deep sleep and gasped for air. After the dream, she realized she could not kill the priest the way she had initially intended, and needed to come up with a better plan—one where she could get away with his murder without a trace.

As her mind wandered, still at odds between her dream reimagined, and reality, Shayla fell back asleep again. Just then, the sound of roaring water briefly woke her up. In a fog she found herself under her bed. She crawled out and the sound suddenly stoped, then started again—this time sounding like the wind blowing through trees. When she turned around, she noticed a tarp covering her bed and climbed in under it. The sound kept getting louder and louder.

She realized it sounds more like water ripping through the woods. Then she had a vision of dogs with their hair on end. She was next looking out her window, trying to see where the noise was coming from.

Then she heard the voice of a man screaming. She got scared and quickly ran back into her bed and under the tarp. She wished the man's voice she just heard was of the priest being killed by someone—*as she further wished it was her.*

Inspired by her dreamscape, and not wanting to forget her conjured ideas for the best way to kill the priest, she instantly determined how she would finally commit this act. *It would be in the woods at night.* There she felt she could get away with murder without leaving a trace. Regaining consciousness, her plan to kill the priest started to unfold in her mind as she beamed a vindictive smile.

It had been a couple of months since Shayla's violent rape attack occurred on the stone table in the patio as she continued her stay for the summer at the priest's house.

As the days and weeks passed, so did the violence increase where the priest made young Shayla his sexual slave—which only fueled her vengeful plan to kill him evermore. She couldn't wait to do it. It had to be done, at all costs.

But when she started to throw up in the garden, the priest's mother realized the young girl could be pregnant. By then, Shayla's cuts and bruises had completely healed and there was no sign of any violence or distress to her physical appearance. The mother knew she had to do something, fast, before this untimely issue could get out of hand.

His mother called her inside and asked her to sit down. It was a small kitchen with a small square table with four chairs. Suddenly struck with déjà-vu, Shayla narrowed her eyes on the shotgun from above the door—as she further recalled being shot in her dream by it. Though realizing she had seen the shotgun before, she never gave it much thought, until the nightmare when she felt the shotgun blow a hole right through her heart.

The priest's mother sat down on the other chair and began to write a note. She then handed Shayla the note and sent her to see the lady who lived down the way. The note read, *"Girl needs help, come to the house."*

When Shayla arrived at the woman's house, she saw she had whiskers on her chin and looked quite scary. She was a very tall woman with only one tooth on the top part of her bridge, a pointed chin with long dark curly wiry hairs. When she smiled, the one tooth gave no indication that hygiene was a top priority. Shayla felt a scary chill go down her spine when she first noticed it, walking back to the priest's house accompanied by the woman with the whiskers.

"Am I pregnant?" she quickly asked.

"Well child, where have you been to be pregnant?" The lady responded with her own question. "What have you been doing? Have you been bad?"

With Shayla's knowledge of adult conversations, from having talked to her next-door neighbor and trusted friend, she said, "The priest fucked me on the patio stone table, and I didn't even cry out loud."

"Be quiet child. Don't ever say that again to anyone. If you ever repeat such a thing, your mother and father will be very mad at you for being a bad girl and they may even give you away to another family." She continued, "Your parents would definitely give you away. No parent wants a daughter who's a puta and fucks the priest."

As Shayla walked with the lady to the house, she never said anything else because now her secret was told to this woman, and she was afraid her plan to kill the priest may not work out.

When they arrived at his mother's house, the two women talked in the kitchen while Shayla waited outside. Then the mother called Shayla inside and asked her to get undressed from the waist down, and to lie on the kitchen table. The woman with the whiskers told her to open her legs while holding a flashlight pointing in Shayla's vagina. She used her spit to lube Shayla's vagina, then she proceeded to insert a long object into her vagina *(later in life, Shayla would learn this object was called a speculum).*

Once the speculum was inserted inside Shayla's vagina, the woman had the priest's mother point the flashlight right into her vagina. She then inserted a coat hanger wire and started poking Shayla's insides right between the walls of the cold object inserted in her body.

"I broke her water," said the woman with the whiskers to the priest's mother. "Now just wait until it all comes out. Get this child home to her family."

Later that day as it started to get dark, Shayla felt severe pains in her lower back area. She was outside curled into a ball in the garden and the priest came over to her. He handed her a wooden box and commanded, "Get in the car."

The unthinkable was about to happen on this dreadful rainy night when he drove her to the cemetery—and young Shayla would be forced to dig a grave in which she would bury her unborn fetus.

Shattered and depleted from her nightmare experience with the priest, her mind became fierce with anger. On her way home after the cemetery, new thoughts of revenge and how she would kill the priest raged throughout her core. She was exploding with hatred toward him for what he did to her. After her cut from the priest's slap at the cemetery had healed, the mother sent Shayla back home to her parents.

Once home she was happy to sleep in her own bed, though woke up many times in the middle of the night, as her sister slept peacefully through the night.

Part of her felt jealous of her sister, for being so calm and innocent, as opposed to herself, so unrested and tainted. However, she never wanted her sister to know her pain. She loved her sister so much, she would suffer it all over again if it meant to save her sister from the same pain and heartbreak. It would break Shayla's heart if her sister, her mother, or father ever knew her pain and her secrets. She was just so glad to be back at home, safe and away from her predator.

Shayla became tough, a front that would be her emotional shield. She forgot all about being a good girl, including her happier times of innocence when she had helped her father work on the farm. Her self-worth lost and shattered, she saw no point in trying to reclaim her stolen youth. *Or to pretend to be that girl anymore.*

CHAPTER 8

Letting Go

Present day.

Emma was hard-pressed to come to terms with Juliette's untimely death. Her one remaining friend from back home on the island was suddenly gone. Emma had opened up to her, entrusted her with her secrets, and the two had commiserated and leaned on each other for support. The events around Juliette's passing had gone from too much too soon, to too little too late. Emma could not let this wake-up call go in vain. She knew Juliette would want her to grow from their visit, to evolve and to heal.

Sometime after Emma had returned home from her trip with her departed friend, she came to a decision. *To make peace with her mother before she passed away.* She also decided to forgive the priest for what he did to her. It was important for Emma to find emotional freedom, a bridge somehow, that would signify her healing and her ultimate, long aspired release from her pain. Her need to be free far outweighed the grievances she had carried throughout most of her life. She had suffered from this heavy burden and secret for far too long and was not going to allow it to rob from her growth any longer.

When Emma's anger would start to peak, she had learned to immediately turn any escalating negativity into love. It took all of fifty years for Emma to learn this technique, a proactive approach that would serve as Emma's roadmap to a freedom-based future. She had further manifested to teach this technique someday to those who saw value in her teachings and wanted to learn from it, *as she had.*

Tired of experiencing the incessant and horrific memory from her dark past every year, she was ready to bury her shame and move past it.

Emma was simply tired of *being tired.* She was tired of hiding from her past. Tired of living a lie. Tired of being angry. Tired of hurting. Tired of living in regret. Tired of suppressing her pain. She wondered how she could love herself past the hurt? How she could love herself beyond her scars? How she could love the woman she had become? She truly wanted to forgive herself for the mistakes she had made in the past due to her fifty years long rebellious streak. She also wanted to forgive herself for hurting the ones she loved, and those who loved her. And she wanted to forgive herself for still so much more... for not speaking the truth, for not telling her parents what the priest did to her, and for leaving her family behind.

Her list of forgiveness wants, *went on...* To forgive herself for making the wrong decisions. For taking so long to realize she was the problem, and for tearing herself apart due her easily-triggered anger. She continued to blame herself for her past actions. She had lived in sheer misery for so long and was finally ready to end her pain. On a mission, she looked for ways to minimize her ache. Though nothing seemed to work at first, she made a vow to finally get rid of her suffering.

She struggled to search for new remedies. She would try different methods to achieve any healing relief. She also went to counseling, though this did little to help her. She didn't know what else to do. She felt like a lost cause. She didn't know who she could run to for help. She prayed and waited for any answers. During her search for healing, she became impatient. Her prayers went unanswered and Emma became depressed. She didn't know what to believe in anymore. Her angst had triggered a deep anxiety and she became suicidal, feeling there was nothing more to live for. Living became even more pointless to her. She couldn't run away from her problems, because they seemed to follow her everywhere she went.

She couldn't tell her husband because he would not understand or relate. She felt all alone and depressed. It was a constant struggle and a cycle she couldn't shake. Every day she woke up to the same nightmare. No one seemed to understand what she was going through or care about her problems. She felt like an outcast to the world—living a double life and hiding her dark secrets. Living a lie to impress her friends came at a cost as she continued to hurt inside. She would put on a happy façade, an impenetrable bluff no one could see through or notice she was otherwise quite the opposite, *in reality.* People would never know her pain and her life-long troubles. The soul of her inner-child had been stolen, creating an empty shell of an existence that she thirsted to fill every day.

Her angst had triggered a deep anxiety and she became suicidal, feeling there was nothing more to live for.

Though she hid her truth from the world to perfection, this daily manipulation ate at her heart and killed her internally. Her soul bled throughout her façade. *She would rather drink her own blood than to reveal her broken heart.* She couldn't talk about her haunted past for fear that people would not understand. She knew they would only judge her, instead of encouraging her. Living in a world where she had to pretend to be someone, other than her true self, broke her to the core. This reality became her new normal. *No illusion.*

With each passing day, it became easier to lie about her fabricated life—*than telling the truth.* She made a vow that she would never allow anyone to know her weakness.

She carried this emotional burden for years, which took a toll on her body. As time passed, her hair started to turn gray, and her body wasn't as strong anymore. The physical effects of aging made her wish she had resolved her anger issues early on in life.

She would do anything to slow down the aging process. She understood there was a time and a reason for everything, and surrendered to what had been out of her control all along.

One particular evening after a long day at work, Emma felt an extreme pull inside her to release her inner darkness. She knew that night was the time she had prayed for toward emotional freedom. Tired from her day, she somehow managed to pull together whatever strength she had left inside her. She made a pot of tea and got into comfortable sweats. She took her prepared cup of tea to her bedroom, where she sat at her dresser desk. She opened the drawer in front and grabbed her stationary. She looked up for a brief moment, as if trying to gather strength and any sign of guidance, then took a deep breath and started to write and write. *First to her father...*

> *To my dearest Father: I miss you tremendously. I miss the days when you were so proud of me. Your beautiful blue eyes smiled upon me when you would see me, and I felt so loved. I remember all the things you have taught me regarding growing vegetables. I cherish the moments we shared. I promise I have not forgotten these cherished times with you. When I see peanuts in the shell, I always remember the day you showed me how peanuts grow and when I see a watermelon on the vine I look to see if its baby is brown before I remove it. I am sincerely sorry I wasn't the daughter who you wanted me to become. Father, please understand I was severely injured to the point that I could not make a sound. I tried to speak but words could not come out of my mouth. I could not speak about my injury.*
>
> *I was threatened to stay silent. I carried this pain in my heart for many years. I apologize it took me so long to come*

out and tell you. I was embarrassed because when I was a teenager, I made decisions you were not proud of. Many years ago, your perception of me was completely wrong. You thought I became a defiant and a rebellious young lady, however the truth is that I was actually paralyzed with fear, pain, and depression. This included suicidal thoughts.

Father, remember the time when you were upset with me because I didn't show up for music lessons? Remember the time I told you I didn't want to go to the priest's house to help his mother? Remember the time I did not come home until dusk after skipping the music lesson and you wanted to know where I had been, and I would not tell you? Remember the night you and mom were waiting for me to come home after choir practice, and I rushed to bed without saying anything?

My dearest father, I am here to tell you why. I was being molested and sexually assaulted by the priest who you loved and honored so much. He tortured me and made me do sexual acts on him.

He also threatened me, repeatedly saying that if I ever said anything he would report to you that I was not a good girl. Like the time he came to our house and asked you to let me go help his mother during summer vacation? That time dear Father he became ever worse as he assaulted, tortured, and raped me on that same night when he picked me up at home. Do you remember telling me to hurry and pack my things and I didn't want to go? Now you know why. I knew I was doomed once I left the house with the priest. I became his captive prisoner at his mother's house.

When I returned to you after the summer stay at his house, I had been beaten, raped, fallen pregnant, and forced to abort my unborn child into a box. Then he told me to dig a hole at the cemetery to bury my own child. You were right in thinking I had become defiant and very disobedient. Though the truth is, Father, that I lost every bit of confidence or respect for myself. I lost trust in people, including those who were supposed to protect me. I wanted to run away to never return. That is why I stayed out late, and I never really cared about what you thought or your house rules.

I am sorry that you have passed away not knowing the person I have become today. Even though I am still in recovery and every day of my life I have to read my affirmations and focus on living a positive lifestyle, I am happy to tell you who I am now. Father, I am kind and I am a wonderful cook just like Mom. I still enjoy growing vegetables and flowers in the garden. I occasionally go for walks in the woods, and I look for beautiful little wildflowers. I have done everything the same way you have taught me. Gentle and with care. I have made great friends along the way. Also, I made peace with people. I have a great life now Father. I am loved by many, and I am highly respected. I am free spirited, and I am still the same person you loved as a child. I have not changed. I still love animals and I enjoy listening to birds chirping in the trees. I love nature very much. When the perennial plants bloom in the spring, I thank them for coming back to see me again.

Thank you, Father, for all that you have done for me. I had the happiest childhood with you. I cherish every moment we shared together. You were a wonderful father, provider, and mentor. I am so grateful that I had you in my childhood years. Believe it or not, Father, I am still your ladybug. Please accept this letter from my heart as a way to confess my wrongs to you. I should have told you about my injuries. I am so sorry, Father, that my actions caused you pain and shame. I honor you with every ounce of my being. Until we meet again, my dearest Father. I love you and always will.

Part of Emma's process for healing was to write letters of forgiveness to her predators—those knowingly (the priest) and unknowingly (her father). She knew the first written letter to her father was only the beginning, and she needed to keep going with her internal release; to the priest as well, who was largely responsible for her pain and suffering.

Following the last word of her letter to her father, she put her pen down briefly and took another deep breath, as preparing herself to write the toughest letter next...

To the village priest: Do you remember driving me home one day after my stay at your mother's house that summer when you tortured and raped me? I was only ten. My parents were happy to see me. They asked if I'd had fun and I told them I did. I lied. You and I both know what really happened then.

I will never forget your violent sexual attacks on my small and underdeveloped body. I was just a child and I did nothing to deserve this. Yet you beat me, raped me and pilfered what was left of my innocence. There was no stopping your repeated attacks and what you started doing to me from the age of nine.

Then when I was only ten, I became pregnant and your mother had a strange lady perform an abortion on me with a wire. Do you remember? I do and I will never forget what you did to me. It has been over fifty years since that last torturous assault and the night in the cemetery when you forced me to dig a grave for my aborted baby. Do you remember slapping me before I fell on the shovel? The scar on my face from the fall on the shovel is a daily reminder of the scars you left in my heart and in my mind.

I remember it all as if it happened yesterday. I will never forget it. The deep wounds I have suffered through as a result of this experience, I've had to deal with every day. Having been assaulted and violated by you has caused me to live a life of deep depression for all these years. However, having lost the love of my father and all the wonderful opportunities I should have had with him is by far worse than any assault.

After all these years, I have carried this heinous memory of what you did to me. You are a vile and pitiful excuse for a man. Despite the many times I have thought of killing you, I could not allow myself to steep to your level.

In my effort to achieve emotional freedom and live a peaceful life, this letter is to set the record straight. It is my release. I realize now the only way I can do that, to be truly free, is to keep moving forward and to not look back. But before I do, it is important for me to call you on what you did to me and to show that I am bigger and stronger than you have ever been.

I will never understand why you did those things to me. However, I am prepared to let go of this memory, as if it never happened. As if you never happened. To release it all. I release you.

He was the priest of the people, a distinguished member of the Catholic Dioceses, a teacher at the local high school, a free tutor for children with learning disabilities, an author, the spotless village hero who was always invited on special occasions by the locals—most his parishioners.

Anytime anyone needed assistance, whether it was legal or financial help, the priest would always help regardless of who it was.

Apart from the other occasions when he had he been accused of sleeping with various women in the village, his reputation was spotless. The people of the church loved him and would even comment that if women wanted it, he would also "give it to them." The priest was truly a *giving* man—in every way. Early on, when Emma was known as Shayla, the time when she was first violated by him, she discovered first-hand the priest's heinous truth. This model citizen showed no mercy to the young who he would prey upon with his violent acts. The priest was indeed capable of so much. God bless the children who didn't comply or tried to cross him. Shayla had regrettably learned that lesson all too well. While she knew the priest was a pedophile, she also realized beyond a doubt that her father would never believe her. She had nothing to prove any accusations she would attempt. For young Shayla, it became evermore clear the time had come to consider other options—either the priest would disappear from her life, or she would disappear from his.

Her truth remained buried from the onset of being attacked by the priest. She could never find the courage or the voice to tell her father what had really happened to her during her youth—something that had haunted her over the forty years that followed her unprecedented ghastly experience with the priest.

Violated since her youth, Shayla had become cold and embittered. She created an emotional barrier between herself and the people around her. It was hard for anyone to get close to her, which suited her just fine. She preferred no closeness from anyone for fear of her past being discovered.

While she knew the priest was a pedophile, she also realized beyond a doubt that her father would never believe her.

It was well into her adult life before Emma could start to love and respect other people, including herself. It was also then when she would start to understand people better, though she didn't believe in love—from others or herself. Her skewed view of relationships, and how she would treat those around her, made her come across as aloof, self-centered, bitchy, selfish, and arrogant; among other preconceived notions. One time a co-worker had even mentioned to Emma that she was like a wild cat: *"You can feed it. You may even be able to let it in the house. But once you touch its tail, it runs away."*

During her youth back at home with her parents, as Shayla, she would tend to her house chores with her mother as if medicine to help ease the torment she had endured from the priest.

Every weekend, typically on Saturdays, the house would get cleaned—the beds would be stripped, the floors would be swept, then scrubbed with a wire hand brush, and rinsed with a rag. All the linens would be washed by hand, rinsed in clean fresh water, then hung on the line to dry. The chores helped to relieve Shayla's mind and her fury.

As an adult, Emma began to contemplate how far she had come—*the moments of her life that would steer her experience forward to the present day*. She reflected on her defiant past. From running red lights and leaving accidents behind, she never looked back to see who she hurt, offended, or disrespected. She never had a sense of loyalty to anyone. She lived for the moment and never had a plan. Now an older adult, she really wanted to change her former ways and stop living recklessly. She recognized the value of life, that hers was too precious and it wasn't too late to start living differently. She really wanted to right the wrongs of her past. *Those she still could.*

Emma further considered how the way she was had impacted her work life as well. She had switched between jobs so often and lived in many places, it was hard to establish any roots or foundation for this rebellious spirit. Although Emma had an education and managed to always have good jobs, including her own house, she wondered if she would ever find true love. She desired someone who would love her unconditionally and not judge her. She began to understand her behaviors and her feelings better over time. It wasn't until years later when Emma began to realize the problem was deep inside her and she had to resolve it somehow. She realized her effort had to start with her long-buried pain, that she had to find healing and needed professional help. This self-discovery was her first step toward recovery and how she would find calm within and acceptance—from herself and others.

Emma would ultimately discover the solution toward self-love. She further relied on close trusted friends from whom she would seek guidance on *how to love*—from giving to receiving it from others. In her learning process within her trusted circle, Emma began to also learn how to love herself.

Like an alcoholic who needs to stay sober, it was important for Emma to stay in a *love mode* mindset and heartset, as well as to temper any remaining deep-rooted anger. She had to also address her scars of trust; the feelings harbored within her inner-well for too long. Emma's resolve was to maintain this balance where she found peace. Her newfound emotional bearing was even stronger than her anger had been—as it began to fade over time. Emma continued to stay healthy as long as her improved mindset was applied to her daily life. While this was not an easy process at first, nor did it feel natural to her, somehow, she was able to make it work with practice and consistency.

As Emma continued to evolve into her newest days with purpose, she discovered her pain and anger had started to fade. She learned how to take hold of her emotions in a way that served her, turning her sadness into joy. She looked at life differently—including nature which helped to relax her and relieve stress. Nature became her sanctuary and her escape, creating feelings of love and warmth. The sounds of nature made her feel safe and serene. Simply listening to a bird's chirp filled her heart with joy. She also loved listening to ocean waves against the surf, providing an added respite for her peace and healing. Just being surrounded by nature lifted her spirits. She so enjoyed the moments when she could lose herself in its poetic embrace.

Emma further enjoyed going on hiking trips which provided a refreshed perspective and clean slate outlook on life—including the discovery of who she truly was, and was not. A new and welcome experience for her, she had not previously realized the true power and peaceful majesty of nature. It was in these moments when she would also learn to love herself unconditionally and let go of her past. It was important to surround herself with positive people. She stopped looking for validation from her peers and continued to shift her mindset.

As she became more accepting of change, she also stopped trying to control everything. She simply didn't care to engage in negative energy. Connecting with her higher-self, she chose to be kinder and stepped out of her comfort zone. She also chose to forgive herself and others as she continued to face her inner obstacles. She accepted where her life had taken her, as she further dealt with old wounds.

She continued to practice the kind of love she aspired to receive and didn't take anything personally. She made peace with her failures and affirmed to continue working on her emotional health as part of reaching her daily goals.

She embraced her flaws and the earlier hardships she had encountered no longer mattered. She was able to finally let go of her past and move forward. Keeping her focus, she didn't allow anything to hinder her healing and growth. She continued to walk into her renewed purpose.

Facing her fears, she accepted the things she could not change as she moved on from her past. She was no longer weak and became stronger with each new day. Her past had no control of her future and could not keep her down.

She made a proactive decision to never look back and to keep moving forward. She stuck to her commitment to let go of her past while also taking responsibility and being accountable for her actions. Spending more time on her self-care and personal growth became a constant in her life. Her efforts ultimately worked and she was finally free of her inner demons, *including her long-held shame.*

Emma made more new friends over the years who adored her. This further included her longtime bond with Lauren, who had supported and nurtured Emma for much of her adult life. While it had taken many years for Lauren to gain her trust, she was the first person who Emma would confide in—revealing her past secrets and pain. Lauren never judged nor commented on Emma's harrowing experience. It was through Lauren's unwavering love and support that got Emma to open up, more and more, as she learned to trust her friend and to believe in love.

The first gift Lauren had given to Emma was a small wooden plaque that read: *"If flowers were friends, I would like to have a bunch just like you."* It took Emma months to believe that statement was true.

CHAPTER 9

Changes

Fifty years in the past.

As Shayla suffered quietly from her trauma with the priest, it directly affected her relationship at home with her parents. Their daughter was suddenly acting differently. During Shayla's teen years, she also became the target of bullying in high school by her classmates. She ultimately became withdrawn, keeping her innermost thoughts and pain to herself. Shayla became so depressed in high school, it permeated into her own self-care. A classmate told her one time that she smelt bad, while pointing to her crotch. This sharing from her friend devasted her and from that point on, she always made a point to wash herself. Other students spoke hateful dismissive words toward her, spouting their disdain with even more cruel digs. They would also spit in her direction when she walked by. All Shayla wanted was to be accepted and loved. However, for all her attempts to fit in, she was rejected instead at every turn.

Adding more sting to her torment, the priest would later take on a job as a teacher at her school. Making matters worse, he became one of *her* teachers. Despite her non-effort in class, and though Shayla never applied herself to study anything, he passed her on every test.

She also lost interest in tending to the farm with her father—a pastime she had so enjoyed with her father as a child. *She was no longer that child.* It would not be long before she also completely stopped helping her mother with house chores. Staying out late and not accompanying her parents to church on Sundays became her new pattern. She wielded her newfound rebellious spirit as a form of empowerment, an entitlement and a license underscoring her "bad girl" behavior.

Considering all she had endured, as *good girl* obeying her elders, she felt like she deserved to act out however she pleased. Now a teen, she was no more *that girl.* Her adolescent misbehaving ways served as an impenetrable shield—where the harsh world that hurt her, and stole her childhood, could no longer get *to her.*

It was hard to miss the pain revealed on her father's face. After all, Shayla's father had gone through the motions of seeing his daughter transformed into someone other than the little girl he had so cherished. She was not the little girl he raised. *Not anymore.* Given what the priest had done to her, she would never be anyone's little girl again—not even to her own parents, for whom she had always done as she was told. It was then, that time of innocence when her nightmare with the priest would begin—and continue to haunt her forever. *The 'good Shayla' had ceased to exist since her first string of attacks, leading to her last, at the hands of her predator. The village priest, as so adored by his church followers, including Shayla's very own parents—devout loyalists to the priest.*

As she grew into her teen years, Shayla became withdrawn and uncontrollable. With a broken heart, her father reached out to the priest asking for advice—as if the break between him and his daughter could be recovered somehow. The whole vicious cycle had turned into a sadistic irony—considering how the father would lean on the priest for his help, *him of all people*—the same evil man who had violently raped his little girl, and was the culprit behind her downward spiral. The father was unaware that his bond with Shayla would never would be as it was, and was forever lost.

Shayla's heart sank when she was in the yard, and saw the priest's car drive up their dirt road. She quickly tried to assess why he was there. A flashback of a similar grave time raced through her mind to that wretched day when the priest had come for young Shayla then; supposedly to have her help with his mother for the summer.

The priest exited his car and lit a cigarette. He looked around for Shayla's father who was working out in the yard. Shayla's father saw the priest and waved him over to where he was. The priest made his approach and the father removed his straw hat as a gesture of respect.

A flashback of a similar grave time raced through her mind to that wretched day when the priest had come for young Shayla then; supposedly to have her help with his mother for the summer...

"Hello Monsignor," greeted her father. "Thank you for coming. How are you?"

"My pleasure," replied the priest. "I heard you were looking for me on Sunday after church."

"Yes, I was. I am hoping you could give me some advice on how to best handle Shayla these days. She has completely stopped talking to me or her mother. She doesn't do any chores around the house, and she refuses to go to church. I can't quite understand her peculiar behavior. And no matter what I tell her or how I reprimand her, she simply doesn't care. I'm afraid she is headed down the wrong path. A few more years like this and she will be labeled as a bad girl, Padre. She will never have a good husband or a family. Her mother and I simply don't know what to do anymore."

Well, sir, here's a thought. Have you considered possibly sending her abroad? Say somewhere far, like maybe Canada. Or even the US."

"No, I have not considered it. Plus, I simply don't have the funds to make a trip like that happen."

"I completely understand. But perhaps I can help you. I could provide the money to facilitate your travel with Shayla to Canada. And because she's only thirteen, she qualifies to be possibly adopted by a family there in Canada."

"I know some people who live in Canada. I can ask them. But how can I repay you for your kind generosity? I may never have enough money to pay you back like that."

"Think of this as a gift and a good deed for Shayla. You won't ever have to pay me back. You can simply provide produce and eggs to my mother, who will surely appreciate it."

After the priest left, Shayla's father talked to his wife that evening about the meeting and together, they planned their daughter's imminent trip.

Shayla's travel to Canada was all set. With the financial assistance from the priest, the father flew with his daughter to the faraway land in search of a better future for her. Once in Canada, and without Shayla around, or to her knowledge, he met with people he knew to discuss his desperate need to find a family that would sponsor his daughter and help her to stay. The search was unsuccessful and a few weeks later they returned to their island home—at which point, Shayla never spoke to her father again. Though she continued to live with her parents and her sister, in her mind she never felt like part of the family. *It was never the same for her.*

Shayla remembered gazing over at her sister, feeling envy for her pure innocence and happiness. She wanted to be close to her sister, but her shame and negative feelings about herself kept her away. Her sister was kind and calm; the total opposite of Shayla.

Wallowing in her dark shell, Shayla felt hopeless and all alone. She couldn't fathom seeing herself continuing her life next to her sister and pretending like everything was fine. Her sister was completely unaware of her pain and suffering.

Shayla was envious of her sister—not as an act of kindness, but of hate. She hated herself and so desperately wanted to be like her sister, more calm and happy, but didn't know how to turn herself around. She could only feel shame and loathsome feelings discounting her own self-worth.

The mere thought of the priest and what he had done to her made her nauseas, triggering incessant feelings that overwhelmed her with hatred for all people. Shayla further battled with feeling love and happiness. Oftentimes she would look at her sister and tried to feel love, but it was like a candle in the wind. Trying to conjure feelings of warmth and love took effort, with little baring as Shayla felt nothing inside her deadened heart.

As time went on, Shayla grew more and more isolated, separated from her sister, as feelings of loss, emptiness and sadness continued to eat into her days. She had received no comfort or compassion from anyone, and she found herself evermore remote and alone. Then one day, the solution occurred to Shayla...

I can remember this day as if it was yesterday. I knew it was what I needed to do. It was time for me to leave the island for good. Just this idea already overwhelmed my heart with joy. I was exploding with excitement. It was finally happening. The moment I had been waiting for—then just magically appeared before me. It was my answer. The only way out of my misery. This was my salvation toward a future that separated me from my past. No one understood my pain or the trauma with the priest that started it all. I could no longer regard my home as Home or feel a connection there. Leaving that place would be the relief I had been hungering for, far too long.

Starting fresh, with a new energy and a life elsewhere, would help me to forget about the attacks from the priest—how he violated my little girl body and the pure essence of my childhood years—turning me into a person I didn't recognize or care to be anymore. I needed to be emotionally free. To heal. To forget. And to truly live again.

I never wanted to look back at those dark memories

that had haunted many sleepless nights. I was so tired of trying to hold in my pain and pretending to be happy. I was tired of feeling ashamed, blaming myself for what happened.

The truth is, I was young and trying to be a good girl, doing as told by my elders. This included my parents who I loved dearly and the evil priest who my parents trusted and leaned on for his guidance—until I discovered, physically first-hand, the truth about this evil monster under the guise of his clergy good samaritan clothing. Because of him, I was violated too young in my growth, and shattered forever. Young or old, nobody has a right to force such acts on another person as if they are their slave. And yet, this was exactly what the priest did to me. I was only nine when it started, and his attacks only continued to escalate from there with more of his violent rapes upon my tiny young girl frame.

I will never forget what he did to me, and repeatedly. There was no mercy from this evil monster. All while my parents continued to trust this animal. Sadly, they didn't know better. I realize this and have since paid that price of their 'not knowing.' At the time, so young, there was nothing I could do, but only as I was told.

I don't care to live this lie anymore, only to please my parents. If they had only known what I went through—just trying to impress them, to be their perfect little girl. Nobody gave me a manual. Nobody briefed me. Nobody said anything to me about being a good little girl, that it meant allowing for naughty vile acts to be performed on my tiny body by the adult priest. I was too young and too naïve. And now looking back, I am filled with remorse that this has even happened to me.

The priest stole my innocence and there is no justice for me. I could never forget what he has taken from me. Plus, he further threatened me to make me remain silent. No one seemed to care about my very existence or that I mattered. I was irrelevant. The more insignificant I felt, the easier it was to remain silent. Through it all however, I am still standing somehow—in spite of all my pain and suffering.

Another big reason why I had to leave that place was so I could feel significant again. The move would signify my solace and give a reassurance for a better and brighter future. I would never forget my family and how much I love them. However, I needed to do what was best for me and my wellbeing.

I wanted to be done with my rebellious ways, all due to my dark past. I was so tired of dying slowly inside. The more I thought about how I was violently raped, the angrier I became. This anger lived within me and festered every day. The priest had created a monster in me, and I couldn't control my rage. It's who I had become as no one heard my cries for help—for all my attempts. That needed to stop. I had to heal. As people didn't see the real me, and all my pain, I didn't care to see them anymore. I had no other choice but to escape to a new life and new hope. I was tired of being upset with myself and the world.

I could no longer allow fear to control me or the better life that I know was still mine to have. Fear had already robbed enough from my past and my youth. I could not permit it into my new life ahead. I didn't know how to fight it before, fear, when I wasn't strong enough and simply too weak at a young age. But I was strong now and reclaiming my life. I was taking back what belonged to me. Me! Otherwise, I would be stuck in a vicious cycle where flashbacks of those haunted memories would remain present, and I could not allow that anymore. I didn't want to keep reliving my past or my pain. Those torturous recollections were lost days that I could now transform into freedom and a fresh start toward better days.

Yes, it was better for me to leave my family before causing them any further pain through my rebellious ways. There was no telling what I was capable of doing. And I didn't trust my anger, still building inside me, where I may have ended up doing something I'd regret.

Tears streaming down her face in her room, Shayla packed her clothes as she struggled to keep a strong front. Despite her heart being wrenched in anger, she still had a soft spot for her family. After all, through it all, they meant the world to her. She knew she would miss them dearly.

Consumed with misgivings about making her trip, even so she knew in her heart it would be for the best. She had to proceed with her plan. The cost of losing her family bared little impact—as on some irretrievable level, she felt that she had already paid that price and there was no going back to how it was between them. Her family could no longer help her. Nor would they ever understand.

I don't trust my anger, still building inside me, where I may end up doing something I may regret.

Having endured so much, Shayla had decidedly come to terms with her ultimate move. At a point of no return, she had to save herself by creating a new life—*far away.* "If you build it, they will come," was the inspiration at the forefront of her mind. It was time to put herself first.

As she left her small bedroom for the last time, her heart gnawed at her to stay. But her mind was made up and she had to go. Shayla had fast-tracked to maturity through her pain as a young child—making her who she had become. Hard and callous, with no concern for hurting the people she loved. She pushed away the ones who loved her the most as her internal fury raged on. She hated who she had become and knew she had to work on healing and releasing her anger. She could no longer hurt her family. *They don't deserve my mistreatment,* she thought. *They deserve better than that from me.*

Shayla hugged her cats one by one and told them she loved them. Feeling her saddest, tears rolled down her face as she tried to remain strong and not show any emotion. She didn't want to leave feeling any weakness. She had to convince herself that she was strong enough to leave the island and to live on her own.

The taxi arrived to pick up Shayla, beeping as it waited outside. It was time for her to go. The house was empty, she looked around for one last time, her sister had already married and didn't live in the house anymore, Shayla had a flashback of her beautiful sister sitting on her bed. She felt so much love and pain, as unsure she would ever see this beautiful farmhouse as her home again. Her departure was emotionally charged with many tears and regret, mixed with acceptance and letting go.

It was now that time—for her to go. Shayla didn't want to keep the taxi waiting and stepped outside carrying her bags. As she walked towards the taxi, she lifted her head and did a sweep of the yard with her eyes. She spotted her father at the far end of the yard working on the farm with his back to the house. Shayla took this as a sign that her father was not open to saying goodbye. She took deep breaths as she walked closer toward the parked taxi. She knew she could do this, despite feeling scared of taking this major leap in her life. *It was either now or never, she thought.* After all, an opportunity like this only comes once in a lifetime. And she was taking it.

The mother walked behind Shayla toward the taxi. As she opened the car door, her mother started to cry hysterically and begged her not to leave, dropping down to her knees in the middle of the dirt paved road and screamed, "Don't leave my beautiful girl! Please Ladybug! Please don't go! I am begging you! My heart is ripping into a million pieces!"

More difficult than Shayla had expected or could have planned, she tried desperately to keep a solid front. Her mind was made up. She had to leave. Staying was no longer an option. She could not bear to look her mother in the eyes. It broke her. There was too much pain and shame for what she had put her parents through. She knew in her heart that leaving was her only path forward.

If only she had confided in her parents about being raped by the priest, would they have believed her then and protected her from him? Would her parents still accept her with open arms? Or would they shun her and push her away?

Unsure what their reactions might have been, not knowing what to trust anymore, it broke Shayla's heart as she realized it was all too late to experience any of those answers. In the end, she realized her parents did their best and could not blame their parenting choices. Including when they subjected her to meeting with the priest, be it for music lessons or helping with his mother—when the nightmare evolved to the next level. And a new Shayla was born.

Without looking back, Shayla quickly jumped into the taxi and told the driver to hurry away. He turned on the engine, but just as he peddled the gas and started to drive away, her mother pulled the door handle and flew it open. Shayla saw the black under her mother's fingernails from working on the farm—a visual of total despair ingrained in her memory that would forever haunt her. Shayla urged the driver to go ahead and keep driving off. Her mother let go of the door handle but quickly tried to grab the black rubber that framed the car window as the car rolled forward. Shayla then saw the top of her mother's black fingernails break off from the pressure of her grip on the thick black rubber around the window.

As the car began to move a bit faster, her mother fell to the ground and grabbed the vehicle's tire in a desperate attempt to stop her daughter from leaving. As the car picked up the pace and drove away, her mother finally gave in to her fight, letting go and falling to the ground limp, weak and broken. As Shayla quickly looked back, she could see blood dripping from her mother's fingertips.

The taxi rolled on and she could not stop crying. She turned around one more time to wave a final goodbye. Her mother's body appeared lifeless, still lying on the dirt road. With that sad parting glance, the car disappeared along the horizon. Shayla could not believe her mother had run after the car like that. *What greater love was there?* From that very moment, she promised to make her mother proud one day, and that she would never break her heart again.

She deserved so much better than the way I had treated her. I hoped one day she would forgive my actions. She raised me better than that, but in my current rebellious state, I knew I was doing what was best for trying to discover who I truly was and recovering any ounce of self-love and forgiveness.

Growing up too fast, I missed out on what could have been a bright, happy and pure childhood. I needed to reclaim my lost inner-child somehow. And my decision to leave was the best thing for me. I never wanted to look back at my haunted past and suffering.

In the taxi, Shayla wiped her tears as she tried to compose her flurry of emotions. Everything was suddenly happening fast. She knew she had to stay focused on preparing for her new life and the journey ahead. Before she wasn't ready mentally, emotionally, or physically. But now, she knew this was truly *her time.*

Shayla's opportunity to grow out of her pain, and far away from her past, was finally here. She put on a tough demeanor and took her new journey to America. When she landed there, she found it to be quite different than her life back home, but somehow managed to adjust perfectly for the time being. She wrote a letter to her mother letting her know she had arrived safely in her transition. Shayla ultimately became a US citizen and continued to hold steadfast to her promise—vowing to make her parents proud.

Though it seemed like she was a million miles away from home, her past still haunted her and the rebel inside was still there. Her spirit still shattered and full of anger, she would disrespect people who tried to get close to her—taking her anger out on them instead. *They did nothing to deserve this, she thought.* She realized her past was still a part of who she was and what she had become, no matter where she called home. That dark period had not let go of its grip on Shayla; as she began to internalize, processing the arc of her new journey so far...

I made some bad decisions of which I am profoundly

ashamed. I am still filled with regret about not only the things I did, but equally, the things I didn't do. I often wonder about how life would have turned out if I had taken more risks. If I boldly said 'yes' to a new opportunity, or made different choices. I mourn all the precious time that has been wasted, turned into lost opportunities. Feelings of regret weigh so heavily deep inside me—I sincerely hope I will heal and overcome it. And the new life I have thirsted for so long is still out there for me to have and to hold with everything I got.

Through all of her troubles and incessant sadness, Shayla's heart and mind were never without the vital inspiration, "Never stop believing."

She knew that if she really wanted something badly enough, she would simply believe with all her might that it would be hers to have someday. She continued to strengthen her mind with empowering visions where she felt love and healing.

As part of dealing with her dark past, she further vowed to always strive for emotional freedom—releasing any negative thoughts with feelings of forgiveness and acceptance. As part of her vow, she was further committed to working her own self-love. She was determined to learn how to love and how to be loved. *I promise myself to truly know love one day.*

It would be years later when Shayla would discover her father had fallen ill. She decided to go back home to see him. It was her unsure attempt at making peace between them. However, upon her arrival when she softly kissed him on the forehead, it wasn't long before she realized he had nothing to say to her. He showed no emotion, nor said a word to her. It was as if she was dead to him—a long-held grievance that had not gone away, no matter the time that had lapsed.

Shayla's father passed away almost one year later. It was then when she would also discover he had completely removed her from his will. Though he was not a wealthy man, he did own land and the family farmhouse. Shayla had long dreamt of having a piece of land that belonged to her father where someday she could visit and reminisce about the days she brought food to her father while he worked. It was the same precious land where he had taught her so much about growing vegetables and how to care for the land with love and gentleness. Silently she wept through the unfortunate revelation that all these years later her father had totally disowned her—not solely from his will, but from his heart.

CHAPTER 10

I Am Shayla

Present day.

The process of healing is powerful on its face—the tell-all reveal where for some, it's hard to miss the pain they have endured written on their face. Everyone heals differently and shows it differently. The process forward is never a straight path. Though making the first step is where it all starts. It takes strength, courage and belief in one's triumph to overcome and become greater than their darkness. Anyone on the road to healing, their impending recovery, can be called a true survivor, if not a hero, for simply doing the work. For the survivor, their walk is never alone. When that glory day comes for those fortunate to experience it, to be truly healed, it's like a symbiotic event—that bolts to the Universe, signifying one's victorious declaration. And in turn, the Universe reverberates that bolt back to the beneficiary with even more illuminated healing.

That moment of true healing had finally arrived for Emma. It was as if the day's luminosity piercing through her window had given way to a hint of its course. She arose that morning feeling refreshed and inspired to truly forget the past. She had gone from falling asleep the night before to waking up with an epiphany of letting go, *for good.* She knew the new day meant a fresh start on life, leading her forward—to never look back or have anything hold her back, ever again. An incredible feeling of power surged throughout her core. She felt invigorated and born again; like she was truly back to her authentic self.

It was like Emma was experiencing an internal celebration at her very core. A long-awaited triumph. She was overjoyed to rediscover the happy little girl who used to run through the fields to greet her father... She *still* had that spark inside her. Now it was suddenly filling her long-lost empty shell with such a powerful surge of love; it felt almost overwhelming to *feel* so much again.

Emma was relieved to finally make peace with herself and her past shame, realizing she had carried this traumatic ball and chain for the last fifty years, far too long, before coming to terms with the fact that what happened had never been her fault.

It was as if a divine source had whispered into her ear:

> *"Healing has always been on the horizon and for you to reach, to have, to hold, and to keep. All you ever needed was a clear-minded focus so you could truly manifest all the healing you've searched for your entire life... simply by putting your intention on your desired outcome every day of your life. From this day forward you are free. Go soar and be happy sweet angel. Never forget to stay in your love-mode mindset... to love yourself and truly feel love. First from you, then to others."*

The road leading up to Emma's newfound joy had been a long one and not without its challenges. For her to finally claim the healing and emotional freedom she had so yearned for was like seeing a bridge in clear sight for the first time, that had been there all along... *hers* to cross when she was ready. Emma had made tremendous progress in her personal journey, simply by taking one brave leap of faith at a time. Before she knew it, she was smiling on the other side of *her bridge.* She had made it!

The time had come to embrace the Shayla she'd tried to bury long ago. She felt safe to be herself again, with no further need for the Emma persona to shield her true identity from the world, especially the precious friends she had allowed into her inner circle. The new day was a beacon to a brighter future where she would be

Shayla, this time, and forever.

It was all coming to a head that day. Shayla could feel it in the air. With incredible new found strength, she knew she was about to embark on a whole other journey, *back to herself.* She was ready for all of it. That included being honest with her dearest friend, Lauren. She had to tell her everything. It was a time of rebirth and no more secrets.

Taking out a pen and writing pad, Shayla started to write down every stage of her life, from her teen years through to her twenties, thirties and forties. The new day signified taking her power back—away from shame and toward freedom.

Shame would no longer rob her from experiencing a fuller life experience. She deserved better. She deserved more. She knew that now, more than ever. *And she was taking action.*

For Shayla, her healing process had become a proactive conviction and a point of no return. She would no longer allow her dark past to hinder her future—something that had already held her back for far too long. She was committed to taking responsibility and being accountable for her actions toward growth. She could no longer allow herself to be the victim in a narrative that only impeded her future. By spending more time on her personal growth, and that which only served her, Shayla was finally emotionally free from her long-held shame. A shame she could see now all too clearly that was brought on by a series of heinous acts committed unto her as a child by her old village priest—the loathsome pedophile where the locals, including her own parents, were none the wiser.

Shayla was a survivor and a warrior, the new badge of triumph she wore proudly. She had endured so much and struggled even more to hide her pain, including her true identity. Tired of running from a past that was beyond her control, she made peace with it all. She had to retire her victimized state of mind. Through her continued self-work and ultimate healing, she was able to address her shame and unleash it back to the person who had injured her. *The priest, her childhood abuser.* By forgiving and releasing her pain back to him, she was also freeing herself in the process. She realized that being a victim was no longer part of her journey.

Through her healing, Shayla further recognized how to steer clear from unexpected triggers that could impact and circumvent her continued growth. She could no longer go back to being angry or self-destructive. Instead, she learned how to gently turn those triggers into self-love and self-respect.

She was sensitive to those touch-points within herself and had learned to be inwardly gentle to stay ahead of any potential triggers. She knew how to stay calm and to not engage in a potentially negative situation. Having come this far, she knew it was far better to just walk away.

Over time she became quite good at saying nothing or simply offering a smile to diffuse an otherwise uncomfortable dilemma. This was her best approach for creating boundaries as part of her effort to stay clear of unwelcome triggers. She now often reminds herself to stay within her bubble; *an imaginary safe place protecting her surroundings.*

This practice reminded her of the precious land owned by her father, who had taught her so much about how to care for it with love and gentleness. She applied the same care and nurturing to herself—becoming her own land and soil, from which to grow.

She had endured so much and struggled even more to hide her pain, including her true identity.

Through more soul searching, Shayla accepted that she was never at fault for what happened. She further started to recognize her true self-worth and potential, a power she had pushed aside along with the past she'd tried so hard to bury. It wasn't until realizing she had always been surrounded by love, that she was able to truly let go and let back in her long-lost self. Like an epiphany, she further realized if she could overcome her trauma, then it was possible for others to do the same. She couldn't be alone in her ordeal and knew she had to share her experience—to bring it all to light so others could find some peace as well. It was important to her to help others find their way toward healing as she had.

Along with forgiving her abuser, Shayla transcended her release to her parents. Had they been more cognizant of her attempted "signs" from childhood—the abuse with the priest could have been prevented. As she had never spoken up, she was on a mission to right the course for others, to enlighten parents to be aware of signs from their children. For they could be in distress and too young to emotionally process or communicate any possible abuse. For Shayla, it had all started from that place of not knowing better, and not trusting that she could come forth to her parents about what had happened to her.

Healing became an ongoing effort for Shayla. She had to keep working harder at it. In her desperate attempt to have peace of mind, her adult years had turned into a lifelong hunt for answers that stretched well into her fifties.

She had to confront her hidden self and see her feelings through. Taking the process further, she read books and consulted with elderly people she knew and could confide in. She further took a close look at her friendships, evaluating every relationship she'd ever had.

When Shayla dug *deeper,* past the surface and the flawless façade that had long masked her private despair, she realized it was her shame that made her hate herself and lead to her fear of rejection. She had lost so much of her life to shame, the demon she allowed to dictate how she would exist in the world—for fear of judgment. Shame became the horrific reminder that kept her moving physically, though she remained crippled emotionally.

Over time and with more effort to heal, Shayla learned that love was stronger than hate. Her desire to truly learn love became so powerful, she was able to accomplish her mission. When she mastered love along her journey, she finally felt the peace in her heart she had been yearning for.

From that point of growth, she started living the life she really wanted—one driven by intentions that served her. As part of her healing, Shayla would travel back in her mind to more peaceful times before she left the island, when she was still a young girl, full of whim and innocence, as she would run through her family farm happy to greet her parents.

Shayla's recall took her to the time when she left the island. Crossing the bridge to her new life was so emotional for her, as images poured through her mind of the drag-down moment when her mother threw herself at the moving taxi cab, taking Shayla to the bridge. Her mother had gripped the vehicle with all her might in her attempt to prevent her daughter from leaving.

The hasty and emotional goodbye between them remained forever wedged in Shayla's mind, traumatic as it felt surreal. She would spend her adult years playing back her escape from the island, feeling remorseful about leaving behind the only life she ever knew, including the family that loved her.

Launching into her new life and identity, as Emma, she made new friends and lasting relationships that would become her inner circle over the years. Though her friends adored her, they only knew her as Emma—the namesake front to buffer her past. Of these friends, one of them included her longtime bond with Lauren; the closest friend who had supported and nurtured Emma for much of her adult life.

While it had taken many years for Lauren to gain her trust, she was the first person who Emma would ultimately confide in—revealing her past secrets and pain. Lauren didn't judge or comment on Emma's harrowing experience; albeit she only knew part of it. She was not told the complete story, yet, and there was still so much more to share. It was through Lauren's unwavering love and support that got Emma to initially open up, more and more, as she learned to trust her friend and to accept the love around her.

With the light of a new day, a freshly spirited Shayla had awakened to new hope and possibility. Her morning stretch filled the air with a certain energy. *Shayla was definitely back.* More than ever, she knew it was time to come forward and reveal everything to Lauren. Shayla was ready for it. She picked up the phone and called her friend.

"Hello," Lauren answered, still reeling from Shayla's earlier breakdown when she had only started to open up to her, without revealing everything. A new emerging Shayla, freed from pent-up emotions, was not going to back down. Not this time.

"Hi Lauren, I need to talk to you," Shayla replied. "Can you meet me at the pond?"

"Which pond? The one you always point out and say someday you'll take me there... *That one?"*

"Yes Lauren, that one! Let's meet there today!"

"Of course. Are you alright?"

"Yes, I'm fine. There's just something important I've been meaning to share with you. I started to tell you before, though I wasn't really ready then and I'm ready now."

"Oh my! I remember something was clearly troubling you. Whatever it is Emma, I am here for you and I will help you through whatever it is."

"Great, Lauren. You always bring me such comfort. You are my closest friend and it's important that I tell you everything. I will meet you at the pond later, say 1 o'clock, okay?"

"Yes dear. That's perfect. I will see you then."

As the women hung up, Shayla became filled with emotion. Excited and anxious, she looked forward to her visit with Lauren that afternoon. Coming forward to her was something Shayla had to do. *Not opening up was no longer an option.* It was time to tell of everything that happened to her back on the island when she was attacked by the priest. Shayla's earlier breakdown and opening up to her friend was only the beginning, but not enough. It was time for the gloves to come off. She had to disclose to her friend once and for all the truth about "who" Shayla truly was.

Heading out the door, Shayla knew it was a threshold to the rest of the healing she had hoped for—there was no turning back now. The pivotal hour that afternoon had come for Shayla to meet Lauren at the pond. What her friend didn't know was Shayla had much more to her story she would further share; *an even bigger revelation.* She braced herself for every detail she needed to disclose to her closest friend. The more Shayla revealed, the more she felt healed.

Driving up to the pond, she parked her car and took a breath as she stepped out. The water reflection gave way to Shayla looking for her friend. Not too far behind, Lauren came into view, making her approach as the women got closer. They hugged, pulled out a blanket and sat waterside.

"How are you my dear," Lauren started. "I'm concerned for you."

Shayla took her by the hand. "Don't worry about me, Lauren. I am fine and actually better now, feeling truly ready to tell you everything about my past when I was just a child and badly hurt. I was severely injured by an abuser. It was my priest back home. I have tried for so long to run away from a past that I had no control over. And I'm tired of running with my soul at half-mast." Tears coming down her face, Shayla couldn't stop there and looked up at her trusted friend.

"Lauren, do you remember when I started talking to you about a friend who was still alive, though I thought she had died... Do you remember? Well, she didn't. She's very much still alive!"

"Of course I do," Lauren offered. "This is why I'm so concerned."

"I will tell you everything. I promise all will become clear to you."

"I love you and I am here for you," consoled Lauren, squeezing Shayla's hands in assurance. "Start anywhere you wish, dear."

Shayla took another deep breath. Then she started...

"Close your eyes Lauren and imagine being in a cemetery..." Just then Shayla looked in her purse and pulled out a letter, a tough one she'd had to write. She opened it and began to read it to Lauren. It was her letter to the priest, releasing her shame.

"To the village priest: Do you remember driving me home one day after my stay at your mother's house that summer when you tortured and raped me...?

Shayla's voice started to fade, and the scene between the two women at the pond suddenly shifted to the gloomy night when she was just a child... and the moon gave way to two silhouettes emerging against its luminescence. This time it was Shayla, older in her present state. She was tentative, holding someone by the hand. It was Lauren by her side, her rock and confidante. With each step taken deeper into the burial grounds by the two women, it was important for Shayla to *show* Lauren what happened, *and where.*

A surreal sequence as if in a dream, Lauren had put her full trust in Shayla who continued to guide her through the faint shadows that blanketed the cemetery. The moon suddenly further illuminated the grave site of that horrific night when Shayla was only a child herself, holding a small wooden box for her unborn, newly aborted fetus.

Fading back to the pond, Shayla continued reading her letter to her trusted friend...

"I will never forget your violent sexual attacks on my small and underdeveloped body. I was just a child and I did nothing to deserve this..."

The surreal sequence at the cemetery faded back into focus. Shayla and Lauren appeared side-by-side, holding each other close. They were peering down at the grave site of Shayla's aborted baby, revealing where it was buried. Just then, with a further shimmer of the moon, it seemed to reflect a blue luminescent flower, *a surreal blue rose,* budding from the foot of the grave.

A feeling came over Shayla that her baby was a boy. In amazement, the women looked closer at the site, then back at each other, tears pouring, and hugged, suddenly struck with a permeating rush of love. There was an inexplicable understanding between the two women. Without saying a word, there was a peace in the misty air. It was clear to Shayla that she was on her path to redemption—the healing she had yearned for her entire life. Finally at a place of self-acceptance, she felt a sense of satisfaction and true release. Her strong desire to move forward took her back to the time when she was a child running freely through the fields, anxious to greet her father.

What her friend didn't know was Shayla had much more to her story she would further share; an even bigger revelation.

Shayla finished reading her letter to Lauren...

"In my effort to achieve emotional freedom and live a peaceful life, this letter is to set the record straight. It is my release..."

Once Shayla had finished reading the letter, she completely let go, crying uncontrollably. Lauren reached for her and held her closer. "My poor, poor dear. There is no judgement here. I'm just shocked and cannot fathom what you had to suffer and carry with you this whole time. I so wish I could make it all go away for you, like this never happened. I have so many questions... While I am trying to understand, there are still parts that I don't understand. I'm just trying to process.

"I have known you for many years and you hid this secret from me. It's just hard for me to believe you are her, not really Emma. You are Shayla! How could this be? How could you be so strong? Do you feel free now? I am so sorry you ever went through this ordeal. It's just so hard to believe this happened when you were so young."

"Lauren, when I came to the US, I changed my entire identity... My name. My whole life had ceased to exist, as Shayla. I didn't want any part of what had been done to her. *To me.* The more I ran away, the more I felt the need to keep going and start my life over. I was prepared to do whatever it took so I could truly forget my past. I hope you can comprehend that, and why I never shared this story with anyone before, until now. I just can't bear to be this façade of my own making, not anymore. I am retiring Emma for good. I just need to deal with who I have never stopped being all along. *Shayla.* This is my only way forward toward true emotional freedom."

"Don't worry, Shayla." Lauren hesitated. "May I call you Shayla?"

"Yes, at this point the gloves are off. So I implore you to please call me Shayla, who I truly am."

Shayla looked her trusted friend in the eye and then jumped up from their blanket and ran into the pond. She started twirling around, raising her arms up in revival glory, a rebirth and jubilation unfolding, stomping her feet wildly through the water.

On some ethereal level, her spirited movement signaled a full circle "coming home" and better days ahead, putting the world on notice—that Shayla was alive and here to stay.

"I am Shayla! I am Shayla! I am Shayla!"

Caught up in all the emotion of her friend's declaration, Lauren was lost for words and began to cry. She was stunned, yet feeling a poetic sense of release and shared rejoice for her friend. She felt the need to simply support and be there for her friend, realizing all further details would fall into place in their own time—whenever Shayla was ready to share more.

Returning from the pond to dry land, Shayla went to sit on the blanket where Lauren waited for her.

"Lauren, I'm sorry for not being upfront with you from the beginning of our friendship. I wasn't ready then and there was still so much pain and healing I needed to process in my own time. I hope you can also understand that I really didn't trust anyone before. There was just so much of my past I needed to conceal. I was so afraid of rejection and being judged by everyone in the new world I had created as Emma. I just couldn't stand being hurt again. I had suffered so much."

"My sweet and precious dear, it's okay," started Lauren. "I really do understand. The story you shared with me is so powerful, it's just so hard to even imagine such a tragedy happened to you so young. It just breaks my heart. But it's going to work out, Shayla.

You will never have to worry about your past ever again, or fear any reprisal from others."

"Thank you, Lauren. Your friendship means the world to me."

"I wish there was something I could do to make all this go away for you. I really do."

"It's all right. I'm a survivor, remember? I just so appreciate you and all your loving support. Now for the first time ever, I can say that I am truly free of this darkness that seemed to overshadow my life. It's like a heavy weight, this longtime burden, has been lifted off from me. I now feel truly free from the pain of my past and all that hurting is starting to fade.

"Now it's time for me to shine and to teach other victims of abuse that they too can do the same! To identify the problem, accept the problem... and to show they have the power to change its outcome! *Yes!* Change it! The *outcome* is all within our power and I intend to keep changing mine for the better! To feel free and alive again... *I am Shayla and I am free!*"

"Again my dear, I completely understand all of it. It's going to be okay, Shayla. There is no need to fret or hide any longer. I am here for you and will help you in any way I can to bring you comfort. I only want you to be at peace."

"Thank you so much, Lauren. Your words and kind heart mean so much to me. I really so appreciate your always being there for me when I need you the most. You are the defining spirit of a true friend. Yes, I am a survivor and I will continue my fight to overcome. But I want you to know that it all started with you and your caring support throughout our relationship. You have helped me in more ways than you will ever know... to discover love, from you to me, and me back to you. I can see now all too clearly that love has always been there for me. And it was you who helped to light that path forward."

Shayla took Lauren by the hand. "There is one more place where I need to take you."

Lauren looked up, revealing her bright blue eyes. "Wait, there's more?"

Shayla beamed a smile as if she had a secret. "Oh, there's more! Come with me."

Taking Lauren by the hand, Shayla led her to her car. The women got in and just as she started the engine, Shayla switched on the radio. The Gary Moore classic, *"I Still Got the Blues for You,"* filled the air. She turns up the volume and started to drive a short distance to an area where the dirt road was covered by overgrown trees. It appeared to be a former campsite by the pond. Beset with intrigue, Lauren looked around but said nothing.

Shayla suddenly stopped the car and jumped out. "I will be right back," she assured Lauren.

She walked to the edge of the pond and picked up a piece of driftwood stuck between some rocks. The driftwood appeared to be part of an old wooden dock, revealing more old wood wedged along the rocks.

In a surreal moment, while the Gary Moore song continued to play, it flowed out from Shayla's car, permeating the grounds with its melody. Swaying poetic to the rhythm, Shayla held the driftwood close to her heart, *a pinnacle moment and moving hint of its significance,* as the song played on.

Curious and concerned about what Shayla was up to now, Lauren jumped out of the car and walked over to her friend.

Shayla turned around. "Lauren, I've been waiting for the right time when I felt truly ready."

"Ready for what?"

"Well actually, it's about a *who,"* corrected Shayla. "There was a girl named Angelina."

Even in her breakdown revelation to Lauren sharing what had happened to her, *with the priest as Shayla,* she was about to reveal even more about the years that followed her earlier adult life in America—including her hidden past with Angelina.

As if her "Shayla" announcement was only a warm-up, Shayla braced herself to tell Lauren everything.

It was important for her to release her truth, *a reveling and coming out,* that further bolstered her newfound emotional freedom. Shayla was more than ever prepared to answer any questions from her friend and would hold nothing back in filling in the missing pieces of her life.

Stunned, amazed, and even more intrigued, simply trying to follow Shayla's mysterious life, as if meeting a new friend for the first time, prompted Lauren's next question...

"Who is Angelina? How does she play a role in your life?"

"It means so much to me Lauren that you are asking, as I am truly ready now to tell you everything more... about this girl named Angelina!"

Her heart pounding, a big smile and twinkle in her eye, Shayla grabbed Lauren's hand with enthusiasm. "Lauren, look around here... What do you see?"

A mystified Lauren looked, confounded by a whole new friend she was suddenly discovering. Everything seemed to be moving fast in all Shayla's excitement and she wanted to be supportive. "I see a pond, an old wooden dock, and what appears to be an abandoned camp site."

Shayla, holding on to her friend's hand, continued her gaze with a smile... as a flashback suddenly came into view revealing a beautiful, serene camp site. An 80s conversion van was parked by the tree line. Just ahead at the end of a beautiful wooden dock appeared two young women sitting dangling their feet in the cold refreshing water.

Still holding Lauren's hand, Shayla lifted their hands up in the air with a gesture of gratitude as she continued to open her arms wide, looking up to the heavens.

"I am so blessed that you have taken a chance on me. You dedicated so much time and love to a girl you hardly knew. You loved me all through my difficult years. Had I only known there was nothing for me to be afraid of and the love I needed was always there."

As they both gave the area one last look, they walked back to the car. In a moment of obscure coincidence, the song Shayla had been singing along with earlier, a Blondie tune, suddenly came back on the radio giving both women the chills. Shayla took Lauren's other hand, now holding both her hands, and looked right into her friend's eyes, blurting out...

I am free!

I want to live!

I have found my voice and my strength—unlike a girl I once knew, named Angelina.

Epilogue

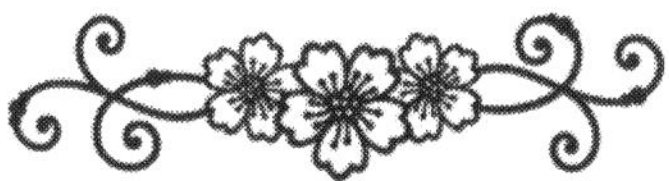

It is a new day for author, Regina LaFrance, a survivor of rape and trauma since her youth. Her present-day experience is committed to emotional freedom and taking her power back—away from the pain, shame and darkness of her past.

So much has already been robbed from LaFrance having a more active, fuller life experience. She knows now, more than ever, she deserves better. *She deserves more.* Unbound by the grip of her childhood nightmare, she is taking action. Starting with her tell-all book, *Shayla,* where she holds nothing back. Not only as part of her own healing process, but for other victims who have suffered from the same dark path and secret.

Keen on making the most her moments, *every moment like she never has before,* LaFrance now flips her life script and leaps off from where she came to all that life has to offer. She feels truly liberated because she has discovered love and her own self-worth—something she had shunned, didn't believe in or considered, since being violated as a young girl.

With the alarming realities of child abuse beyond belief, it is Regina's mission to keep raising awareness for people raising children. Her fight is to prevent the unthinkable from happening; *as it did to her.* "A light needs to be shed considerably on this tragic abuse epidemic and we need to do everything within our power to protect our precious young and innocent."

LaFrance's story is one of the too many who have suffered. And when one suffers, "we all suffer." Her story is their story—a voice for the *frightened little voices.*

If you have been the victim of abuse, exploitation, or neglect, you are not alone. Many people care and can help. Please tell your doctor, a friend, or a trusted family member.

Also consider these resources:

National Help Hotline
800.656.HOPE (4673)

RAINN (Rape, Abuse & Incest National Network)
www.rainn.org

NSVRC (National Sexual Violence Resource Center)
www.nsvrc.org

NCTSN (National Child Traumatic Stress Network)
www.nctsn.org

FIGHT FOR JUSTICE

Author Regina LaFrance has commenced to take steps with the church from her former village in Southwestern Europe; seeking justice for all her hardship and loss of quality of life directly affected as a result of her unimaginable ordeal at the hands of her old priest, a pedophile. Issued as a sworn statement, her formal declaration outlines the grievous events of her young life when she was violated by the priest as he raped, impregnated and held her captive in his mother's home.

When LaFrance issued her sworn statement to the church with a demand for justice for all her trauma, she was shunned and disregarded so soon in her attempt to be heard. Nonetheless, her fight remains unwavering. Instead of being compensated for the sins committed by the priest, the church has formed a committee of experts and shrinks; offering contradictory free counselling to not only the victims, *but to the abusers as well.*

"It makes me sick to my stomach that they didn't as much as address my sworn statement. What about me and what I was put through by one of the church's very own, my former priest? What about my youth that was robbed from me? I will never have that back! Never! Where is my justice that I deserve?" — REGINA LAFRANCE

The release of her book, ***Shayla***, marks only the beginning of the author's fight for all her suffering. It is her mission to keep raising awareness and to put a spotlight on this prevalent issue of abuse within the church.

LaFrance's book is a calling out and a demand for justice.
Join her fight.

BONUS CLOSING SECTION

THE LAST SECTION OF THIS BOOK FEATURES OUTTAKES FROM REGINA LAFRANCE'S SWORN STATEMENT… HIGHLIGHING AND RECAPTURING THE ACTUAL HORRIFIC EVENTS OF HER YOUTH, WHEN HER NIGHTMARE STARTED TO ESCALATE AT THE MERCILESS HANDS OF HER PEDOPHILE PRIEST; MARKING ONLY THE BEGINNING OF HER BRUTAL DEFLOWERING.

TURN THE PAGE…

WHERE LAFRANCE HOLDS NOTHING BACK REVEALING THE "REAL EVENTS" THAT INSPIRED *SHAYLA.*

Sworn Statement

Direct Outtakes from Author
REGINA LAFRANCE

As part of author Regina LaFrance's ongoing mission and fight for justice, she has released a sworn statement about the specific events as they have unfolded from her youth; the dark period of her life when she irrevocably succumbed to being violently and repeatedly raped by the pedophile priest from her old village.

I, **Maria Regina LaFrance**, do SOLEMNLY AFFIRM AND SAY THAT:

> *I have lived my life from the time I was 10 years old with a dark secret that has eaten me alive. This secret has traumatized me, and it has paralyzed me with shame and fear of being blamed and judged...*

[FOLLOWING BELOW FROM LAFRANCE'S SWORN STATEMENT INCLUDE DETAILED SEXUAL ACTIVITY NOT SUITABLE FOR UNDERAGED READING]

When Everything Changed

In the Priest's Car

- I remember everyone piling up into the priest's car. I always sat on someone's lap because I was so small. My house was the closest to the church. If the priest dropped me off first, I would have been home before anyone, but the priest always drove past my house and dropped me off last.

- At first, I was happy to go for the longer ride as it was not very often that a child had the opportunity to ride in an automobile with a group of adults.

Alone in the Priest's Car

- One rainy evening, the priest had everyone in his car. I remember him having a cigarette hanging from the side of his mouth. He dropped off every person from the choir practice at their homes.

- When the priest started to drive away from the last drop-off, he reached to the back seat with his hand and touched my leg. I pressed myself as far as I could against the car door behind the driver's seat, but he could still reach my leg. He rubbed my legs up and down a few times. I remember him saying,

"*Move over to the middle of the seat.*" I replied, "*No, I'm just fine here.*"

Then he said, "*Come on over to the middle. Don't be afraid, I just want to see you better.*"

I said, "*No, it's okay,*" and pressed my body even harder towards the car door.

Once we got to my house, the priest stopped the car and said, "*It's raining, jump over to the front seat and wait here until the rain stops.*"

- The priest then reached over to where I was in the backseat, and before I had a chance to open the car door and run out, he pulled me towards the middle of the backseat. The priest faced forward as a crack in the front driver's window opened. He then lit a cigarette with his left hand while he held me on the seat with his right hand.

- He did not move his hand up or down, he just gripped my knee with his hand. I was not free to go. I was confused and unsure what to expect as I had never been alone with a man in a car like this.

- The priest continued to hold me by the knee, and with one finger rubbed my skin in small circular motions. I managed to pull away, but he grasped my knee again and I remember him saying,

  "*Not yet it's still raining, you have to wait.*"

  I said, "*But I want to go home. My parents are waiting for me. I can run in the rain.*"

- The priest finished smoking and then threw the lit tip of the cigarette out the window and I remember him saying,

  "*Go home. I only kept you here because of the rain. Your parents would be terribly upset if you got sick by walking in the rain.*"

- I slid to the side of the seat and quickly opened the car door.

I ran home as fast as I could and never looked back.

- I was scared and confused. I never told my parents that the priest touched my leg and held me in the car by grabbing my knee. I thought about it all night. I wanted to tell my mother, but I did not want my mother to be mad at me.

- The following week when it was time to go to choir practice, the choir members picked me up at my house and we all walked to church.

- When the practice was over, the five or six choir members that needed to be driven home piled up into the priest's car and the drop-offs began. Again, the priest drove right past my house and dropped everyone off at their homes first.

- On the way back he reached to the back seat and touched my leg. I moved over to the far side near the door, this time behind the passenger seat making it a bit more difficult for him to reach. When he noticed that I was sitting on the other side and not behind him, he stopped the car on the side of the road. He turned around to look at me. I remember him saying,

  "Jump over to the front seat."

  "Why?" I replied. *"Because you can sit in the front seat, like a big girl,"* he said.

  I replied, "*No, I don't want to sit in the front seat. I want to go home.*"

  He then said, *"I'll drive you home for sure, but it's still early."*

- At this time, I opened the car door, and I ran out of the car as fast as I could and hid in the bushes. It was dark out and I was so tiny, I thought he would not be able to find me, unless he had a flashlight. I heard him come out of the car and call my name. I remember him saying,

  "Regina, come on out of there, don't be silly. I am not going to hurt you in any way. I'll drive you home."

- I made a noise while attempting to hide further into the bushes, but he heard it and walked towards me. He grabbed my hair and pulled me out of the bushes. He then held me by my arm and guided me back into the car to the front seat.

- Once inside the car, he told me to stay still, or he would tell my father I misbehaved. Then he went around the driver's side of the car, lit a cigarette, and began driving towards my house. While he was driving, he reached over to my seat, and touched my legs, this time touching my inner-thighs. I remember him saying,
  "Do you have hair there?"

- I did not reply or say anything else. He then grabbed my inner-thigh. I remember him repeating,
  "Do you have hair there, I asked you!"

- This time he grabbed my small skinny inner-thigh leg with force, and I replied,
  "I don't know."

The Priest's Pants Zipper

- Suddenly the priest grabbed my arm and pulled me next to him while he drove. He took my hand and placed it on top of the zipper of his pants. I felt a big and hard thing in his pants with my hand. I remember him asking,
  "Do you want to see it?"
  I replied, *"I want to go home. My parents are waiting for me."*

- We then arrived at the end of the dirt road where my house was and he released me. I remember him saying,
  "Now, go on home and tell your parents you were a good girl. You know they always ask me if you were good. I will tell them again that you were a good girl. You do not want to make your father angry, do you? And you do not want your mother to be sad, do you?"

- I scooted over to the car door and opened it. Once again, I ran to the house as fast as I could without looking back to see if the car was still there.

- I knew it was wrong for a man to want to touch a little girl and it did not feel right. I also knew it was wrong for a man to put my hand over his private area. My father was the only man I had ever been near, and he was a respectful man; he would never touch me or my sister in any way like that. From that day on, I was afraid to go to choir practice.

More of Everything Started to Change

- I told my mother I did not want to go to choir practice anymore. However, my mother made me go. She told me it was good to give back to the church, as we were poor and could not give a lot of money. Being in the choir and participating in the church activities was a way of giving back to the church. I remember the conversation with my mother,

  "But Mother, I don't like going."

  My mother said, *"You must go, Maria Regina, it's good for you to go and I like when you sing in the church; you sound so beautiful, and I'm so proud of you."*

  I replied, *"But Mother... I just don't like it, and I don't enjoy it."* She said, *"Your father is also very proud of you. He is so happy that you're being such a good girl."*

- I remember my mother saying with a stern voice,

  "I don't want to talk about this again. Your father wants you to be involved with the church, and this is a good way to keep you focused and give you an activity to do. You do not want to disappoint your father, do you?"

- The following week when choir practice was over, I contemplated walking home, but I quickly changed my mind when I realized it was dark and I was afraid of the dark. Also, on the way to my house from the church, there was a family that had several guard dogs that were loose at night. I had heard adults talking about those dogs. The dogs would come out to the street and bark at anyone that got close to the property. I was afraid that the dogs would attack me.

- After choir practice, I wanted to be the first one to be dropped off, but I knew the priest would never drop me off first. My throat would become tight, and I could not speak, so I looked out the car window at the moon and stared into the night as the time came when the last passenger was dropped off. I knew what came next.

- Moment by moment, the terrifying threat of being alone with him intensified as I knew within minutes, he would ask me to move on to the front seat, and he would tell me if I did not, he would tell my father I was bad.

The Second Zipper Incident—Priest Ejaculation Sighs

- The priest drove as fast as he could to drop off the choir members but when he was alone with me, he slowed down. Once the car turned the corner, he slowed the vehicle down and as I had feared, told me to move to the front seat. I remember him saying,

  "Move on to the front seat, do I have to tell you every time?"

  I replied, *"I'm fine here. My parents are waiting for me. I want to go home."*

  The priest said, *"Your father has asked me if you're a good girl. If you don't move to the front seat, I will tell your father that you're not a good girl."*

- The priest reached to the back seat and grabbed my knee forcibly as I tried to move over behind the passenger front seat against the car door. He pulled me towards the middle and stopped the vehicle. He turned around and grabbed me with both hands and I remember him saying,

  "You must do your duty; you must be a good girl and you know what you have to do."

- He pulled me to the front seat next to him. He unzipped his pants with his left hand and with his right arm around me, pulled me towards him, pressed tight against his body.

- He then took my hand in his and he placed it around his erect penis, and he began to stroke it. I had my eyes closed and I pretended I was walking through the woods collecting wildflowers to bring home for my mother's table.

- My throat was tight, and I was unable to speak. The vision of picking flowers through the woods was like watching a slideshow behind my eyes, and it assisted me in not paying any attention to what the priest was doing with my hand.

- Suddenly the priest let out a big yelp followed by a big sigh, and I felt my hand all wet and slimy. The priest took my hand, and he rubbed it on his underwear as if he was cleaning it. Then he pushed me away to the passenger seat towards the door. I remember him saying,

  "Now, that's a good girl. I will tell your father you were a good girl."

- I did not say anything to him. I opened the car door, and I ran home as fast as I could.

Hiding in the Woods

- The only thing my parents did not know was that I was afraid of the priest, so when it was time to go to practice to learn how to play the mandolin, I hid in the woods. I hoped the priest would not come to our house looking for me.

- I waited in anxious silence for long periods of time in a safe place in the woods down the road from my house where I could see the only afternoon bus go by, around 4:30 PM. I went home once the bus passed by because that was the time I was expected home.

- One day I fell asleep in the woods while waiting for the bus to go by. I did not wake up until dusk. When I got home, the priest was there. I presumed my parents had alerted him that I never came home. The priest was showing his concern for my disappearance, and he told my parents that I never showed up for any music lessons.

- My parents demanded that I tell them where I had been, but I could not speak, my throat was tight, and no words would come out. I remember feeling paralyzed from my nose down. I wanted to talk, but no words would come out.

- My parents were embarrassed and they apologized to the priest for my actions. They assured the priest that I would be going to the music lesson the following day and that I would also be sent to confession the following Sunday before the church services.

- When the priest left our house that day, my parents sat me down and asked me where I had been going all those days that I was supposed to be at the music lessons. I could not talk about it to my parents because I did not want my father to think I was not a good girl. After many unsuccessful attempts to find out where I had been going, my parents dismissed me and sent me to bed.

The Music Lessons

- From that day forward my parents made sure that I went to the music lessons on the designated day. Every time I went to the lesson, the priest sat me next to him in the sacristy. He would put his arm over my shoulder, showing me how to hold the mandolin properly by placing the far end of the instrument over my tiny chest area, where he then placed his hand right over it. He then proceeded to place his hand under my dress through the neck opening. Since his hands were large and the opening of my dress was small, he would touch my nipples with the tips of his fingers.

- At this time, I was almost ten years old; I did not have developed breasts or big nipples, but I was starting to develop tiny breasts. I remember that they were extremely sensitive and sore when they were squeezed.

- This priest had no reservations about squeezing my tiny breast area. He made sure I did not say anything or pull away. While he held me tight against his body, he talked about learning how to play the instrument and squeezed my tiny breasts with his fingers. I remember it hurting so much. One time I tried to pull away and he immediately pulled me back with such force that it made me afraid to say anything after that.

- During music lessons the priest never took my hand and placed it over his penis. He also never unzipped his pants which gave me some relief, but I still did not want to be there, and I did not want to learn how to play the instrument.

- The music lessons went on for about six months. I never learned how to play the mandolin and I remember my parents talking about it. They told me several times that they were surprised that I never learned how to play because I was very smart, and I could learn so many other things. I remember telling my mother that I hated learning how to play the mandolin and that I was never going to learn.

Going Home After Choir Practice—Masturbation

- I attended choir practice for about one year. Each time he drove the choir members home after practice, he would always dropped me off last and he physically pulled me to the front seat and told me to do my duty which consisted of him masturbating with my hand under his hand until he ejaculated.

- The first few times he had me hold his penis, he would then place his hand over mine and stroke it until he ejaculated, but then he moved on, making me stroke his penis without his hand and he would tell me to do it faster or slower.

Pushing My Face Down on His Penis

- Then he started pushing my head down to his lap. While I was stroking his penis, he would push my head until my face touched his penis. Pushing my face down and rubbing my face on his penis happened many times after choir practice, but I don't remember how many.

One Night—Bleeding

- One night the priest forced his penis in my mouth deep in my throat. He told me to open my mouth and he shoved his penis in it by pushing down on my head. His penis was very erect, and it was so thick that both ends of my mouth ripped and started to bleed. I started to make noises of discomfort and I struggled to pull away, but he did not let me. The more I struggled to pull away, the more he moved my head up and down with both of his hands.

- While he was ejaculating, he let out the loudest sign of relief. When he was finished, he quickly pushed me away towards the other side of the front seat. He reached for a cigarette while he pulled his pants up. As he reached for the cigarette, I was gagging and started to vomit; he told me to open the car door and not dirty his car.

- I was unaware that the sides of my mouth were bleeding. It hurt badly. I was in total shock and confusion. While I was vomiting, still sitting in the passenger seat with the door opened, he told me to go home and wash my face. He told me to go to sleep and if my parents asked me if I was a good girl, to tell them I was a good girl and that the priest said I was doing really well in choir, and that it would not be long until I was playing the mandolin at church services.

- He told me to close the car door and then drove away while I walked home through the short dirt path leading to my house. I placed my hair in front of each side of my face to cover up any signs of distress to my face. When I got home, my parents were sitting at the table playing cards. As I expected they asked me if I had behaved at choir practice, and I told them yes.

The Next Morning

- I remember getting up the next morning and feeling pains on each side of my mouth, it felt dry and sore. I was afraid my mother would see it and ask me what had happened.

- When I got up, I quickly made my way to the only mirror in the house above the wash stand, and stepped on the small wooden box my father had made for me to use as a stepping stool to be able to see my face in the mirror.

- I then saw dry blood around my lips. I saw the rips that the priest's large penis had caused. I dipped my hands in the water in the hand wash bowl on top of the wash stand and I washed my face. I covered the sides of my face with my hair so my mother would not notice. And that was okay, because I always had my hair down and my mother knew I did not like to pull my hair back. So at least I did not have to explain why I had my face covered.

- I thought that my life could not get any worse, but it did.

The Priest Asking for My Help with His Elderly Mother During the Summer

- On the first day of summer vacation, the priest showed up at my house and asked to speak with my father in private. I was playing in the yard when I heard a car pull up through the dirt road. I immediately knew it was him. He drove a black car that read "Simca" on it. I will never forget it because it was in this car where I had been violated and attacked in more ways than I will ever be able to describe. I hid behind the stone wall, and I could hear the two of them talking.

- The priest greeted my father with a handshake and said, *"How are you Senior Paim?"*

  My father replied, *"As you can see working in this heat, Senior Padre. What can I do for you?"*

  The priest then said, *"Well, as you know, my mother is elderly now and I'm very busy at the church. She requested if you and your wife would allow Regina to spend some time this summer with my mother to keep her company?"*

  "Of course," my father said without hesitation, *"Whatever you and your mother need, if we can help, we will."*

- Shortly after that conversation between my father and the priest, I remember my father calling me and saying,

  "Go pack some clothes daughter; you are going to stay at the priest's house to help his mother for a while this summer."

- My father spoke with such confidence and authority that there was no pleading with him. When he spoke, I did as he told me.

  "Do as Senior Padre and his mother say. Do not be an embarrassment to me! You are a special, smart girl, daughter. The mother of Senior Padre has requested you to help her during school vacation, and it is a good opportunity for you girl. Just consider yourself lucky to be the chosen one; then you don't have to help me on the farm."

- My face was serious with my dark long curly hair covering my cheeks. I looked up at my father and I pleaded with him not to let me go. I was pulling any excuse I could come up with to create a valid reason not to go. I told my father that I had promised my mother to help her in the kitchen; that I wanted to learn how to crochet a new pattern for a scarf. I also told my father I enjoyed being with him on the farm and I really did not want to go.

- I was so frightened that my heart was beating very fast. My father then told me to go pack some clothes, that I would be going to help the priest's mother.

- I lost every bit of energy in my body. I considered laying down on the ground and fake fainting, but my father insisted that I gather some clothes to go help the lady who we knew well; a very sweet woman.

- I wore a cute little dress the local seamstress, a woman named Adelaide, had made for me. I looked up at my father with my dried soft pink lips in a big panic, perplexed and surprised look, and with a last-ditch effort I remember pleading,

  "Father, I am afraid. I do not want to leave you, I want to stay with you all summer and work with you on the farm. I never want to leave you. Please do not let me go, please Father, do not let me go."

  My father replied, *"Don't be silly daughter, you will enjoy it. The mother of the priest is very sweet, and she will see that you will have a good time."*

- I was not prepared for this and was caught off-guard. I kept saying anything that came to mind in a plea not to go. While this conversation was going on with my father, the priest looked at me while he smoked a cigarette; looking like he was enjoying my fright looking at my father while he spoke.

- The priest stood a bit to the side, and I threw a worried look over at him and then back at my father. I was so afraid to leave, but had no choice. I went to the door of my small bedroom at the back of the house, and I froze in fear while my father ordered me to gather some clothes to take with me.

- I knew what I was feeling was not right. It was not right for a child to be forced to leave her father's side in fear. This was big, bigger than any other feeling I had ever known. It was a feeling of tightness in my chest, a bellyache, dizziness, and a sense that something terrifying was going to happen to me.

- These feelings were very frightening, and I was once again frozen in a state of confusion to be alone with the priest. I remember hearing my father call my name again,

  "Regina, hurry up, you should never make anyone wait for you! You know how I feel about that."

Arriving at the Priest's House

- When we arrived at the priest's house, he kept me in his office which was next to the right side of the front door. He never brought me down to the kitchen to meet his mother and he signaled with a finger in front of his mouth for me to be quiet.

- I stayed in his office quietly until it was dark, then he came near me and suddenly grabbed my very small, tender, newly developed breasts and squeezed them. At this time my breasts were no bigger than a cherry.

- I did not cry or make any sound; he then slapped me across my face and I fell to the floor. I quickly brought my hand to my face to make it feel better. He then ordered me to get up and to walk outside. Once we were outside, he walked behind me and directed me to go to the back yard.

The Backyard at the Priest's House

- The priest guided me down the outside stairs, passed through the kitchen door and once we got to the patio area, he slapped me again and I fell to the ground. He reached down, picked me up with his left hand and slapped me again across the face with his right hand. The slap to the face this time pushed me against the stone wall forcefully and I fell to the ground again.

- A feeling of terror came over me and I closed my eyes. My arms felt limp beside my little body, I was lightheaded and at that very moment I believed I was having an encounter with death. I felt no strength or desire to keep fighting; it was over, he had won.

- Then, I opened my eyes and realized I was not dead. I felt no pain. I got up and just as I had planned to run around him, he grabbed me by the bottom end of my dress, and he pulled me towards him. I pushed him away, but he pulled me so forcefully towards him that my dress ripped and a piece tore off. He stood there holding a piece of my ripped dress in his hand and a cigarette hanging from the side of his mouth.

- I was in a state of shock, possibly even numbness and I allowed my body to just fall to the ground. I crawled to the stone wall where I thought I could possibly hide. I remember I bent my knees and sat on the ground with my long hair covering my small body for protection.

- He lit another cigarette, and smoked while he stood over me. The moon gave enough light that I could see everything he was doing. I recall him saying while he smoked a cigarette,

  "Remember all those times that you got away; all those times that you didn't show up for your music lessons? You should have been a good girl and done what you were told."

- I did not say a word and instead looked up at him, anticipating another blow to my face. He dropped the piece of torn dress he had in his hand and walked towards me by the stone wall. He grabbed me by my hair and picked me up. He let go of my hair, but quickly grabbed me by the arm and spun me around to the middle of the patio area where there was an old stone table.

On the Patio Stone Table

- He ordered me take off the rest of the torn dress and the pale-colored underwear that matched my torn dress; that was also handmade by the local seamstress. I was frozen with fear and was not able to do as he said. He violently pulled the remainder of the torn dress off of me and then ripped my pale-colored underwear off my body. With one harsh pull of my arm, he laid me on the stone table next to him.

- While he sucked on his cigarette, I laid on the cold surface completely naked and covered in blood from the scrapes and dirt from the ground. He ran his hands down between my legs and touched on the soft fussy area of my private. With his other hand he unzipped his pants, took out his penis from his pants and rubbed it on my private area. It was so hard it felt like it could burst at any time. He then penetrated my private area with his fingers. I held my breath as I was in the utmost pain, shame, and in complete loss of hope.

"Cry Little Cockroach, Cry!"

- He next spat on his hand and rubbed my private area creating a moist spot, then forced his hard stiff penis into my private. He stuck his fingers in my mouth and motioned in and out of my mouth with his fingers as he did with his penis in my private area. Both sides of my mouth ripped as he stuck more than one finger down my mouth, and blood started dripping down my chin; further dripping onto the stone table as he continued saying, *"Cry little cockroach, cry..."*

- But I never cried as I laid there in extreme pain as he was violently raping me. My mouth and my vagina were now bleeding from the attack, and I fell in and out of consciousness. At this time, I was a child at the mere age of only 10; *but I remember it all as if it was today!* It was the most horrific experience a child could ever endure.

- I may have gone into an unconscious state because I remember not only the experience so vividly as if it was today, but also I further remember the visions I had as my internal escape and mental buffer from what was happening. I could smell concord grapes on the vine. I could taste the grapes as drifting away from the pain I felt. I imagined the grapes bursting in my mouth with the soft scent I could smell. I saw myself running through a vineyard, with a view of the ocean from my father's farm. In my imagination, I could hear the affectionate voice of my father saying,
  "Daughter, make sure you do not step on the grapes."
  "Yes Father, I can run fast and not step on the grapes."
  "You're a good girl, daughter."

- I imagined myself running through the field of grapevines, avoiding the areas where the leaves are thick just in case there were grapes beneath the leaves. As I felt a stream of tears pouring from my eyes, I continued to imagine watering the vines so they would produce better grapes for my father to make wine with.

- Suddenly I had a vision of people having sexual relations as I had seen in a magazine I inadvertently found just the year before; that was brought home by a soldier neighbor, and I then realized the same thing was suddenly happening to me in the priest's back yard.

- The pain was horrible and the burning sensation in my

private area was so intense I woke up from the beautiful imagined site of running towards my father in the vineyard. My eyes were closed, my body was motionless, covered in dirt and blood.

- The priest was still pushing his erect penis into my body faster and deeper; when I had gained consciousness again and became aware of my surroundings. In a state of shock as I realized all over again what was happening, I became enraged and opened my eyes.

- I saw the priest with his back to the house and his eyes open looking at me. He appeared to be smirking at me with great pleasure. I shivered in horrified anticipation of his penis going back into my vagina, with more in-and-out motion as he enjoyed my dread.

Feeling Ready to Die

- Suddenly he shoved his penis inside me roughly pushing as hard, and as far in as he could, further intensifying my pain. I began to bleed profusely and closed my eyes because I was ready to die. I remember thinking I wanted to die with my eyes closed.

- He continued to brutally shove his penis again and again until he spurted his sperm inside me, grinning with triumph and pleasure until he was drained and dry. I must have closed my eyes, because I remember opening my eyes again and I watched him pull up his pants that had fallen to his knees. He then zipped his pants and reached for a cigarette, lit it and walked away.

The Priest's Mother

- There was a dim light above the door on the patio in the back of the house. After a brief state of confusion, I looked at the door and to my surprise, the door opened and the priest's mother came out holding a sheet.

- She helped me to get up. She put the sheet over me and told me to go inside. I stumbled a few times. She helped me every time I stumbled. The priest's mother guided me inside, then gave me a wet towel to clean myself and told me to go to sleep. I did not go to sleep. Instead, I laid awake in pain.

- I then heard voices coming from the other side of the house. I attempted to get up and tippy-toe to the door. I opened the door as I heard the priest's mother yelling at him. I heard her telling him that he had crossed the line. She told him that what he did was unforgiveable and if he ever touched "that child" again, she would report him herself.

- She also told him that Regina was only a small child and that he did not have the right to start doing "to her" what he had done to Juliette.

- The priest did not speak a word. I heard her tell him, that messing around with women is one thing, but to hurt a child the way he did, was something she would never tolerate.

- The priest's mother was a sweet tiny lady. She cared for me.

- She assured me that what her son had done would never happen again. She cared for my cuts and bruises and within a couple of weeks nobody would ever know that such a thing had happened.

- I think several weeks had passed. I asked her to go home, that I missed my parents. She assured me that I would be going home soon. Unfortunately for me, I started feeling sick to my stomach and was suddenly throwing up every morning. The priest's mother was usually in the kitchen; she must have seen me throwing up in the garden of the back yard. She called me inside and asked how I was feeling. I told her I was not feeling well every morning.

On the Kitchen Table

- She immediately telephoned someone and before I even knew what was happening, a woman arrived at the house, told me to lay on the kitchen table and to take my pants down.

- I had no idea what was about to happen next as I tried to figure it all out. The woman inserted something in my private area. It felt like I was being raped all over again, but this time with an object by a strange old woman. I remember this lady telling the priest's mother,
  "I broke her water. Now you just have to wait."

- The old woman left and that evening I was curled up into a ball in the backyard with severe pains in my lower back and crying. The priest's mother came out and told me I would be going home in a couple of days. She again assured me that her son would never touch me again.

- The pains in my lower back intensified and I felt like something was about to pass through my private area. The priest's mother handed me a small wooden box and told me to squat over it, which I did. A rush of stuff came out of my body into the box. She called her son, the priest, and instructed him to drive me with the box to the cemetery after dark.

- That night the priest ordered me to get in his Simca car. He then drove to the local cemetery next to the church. Upon our arrival, he told me to get out of the car, go to the cemetery shed, grab a shovel, and then to start digging a hole in the area where infants were buried.

- He stood smoking, watching at a distance. Once I dug a hole the priest told me to place the box in it and then cover it up. I was weak and shaking.

- I remember being so afraid as I thought about death and how much pain it takes to die. The confusion and torture I was experiencing made me cry out loud.

- The priest rushed over to where I was and slapped me across the face so forcibly that I fell to the ground. He told me that if I did not stay quiet, he would tell my father I was a bad girl. I buried my face in my hands and I sobbed.

- At this time, I looked up at him and yelled,
  "You disgust me! I curse you! I detest you!"

- He immediately walked over to me and swung his hand across my face so hard that I stumbled and fell to the ground on top of the freshly dug grave. I hit my face on the edge of the shovel that was still lying there. I felt the sting of flesh and knew I had cut myself. I remember thinking, *"I am not dead."* I could smell the dirt as I felt my cut burning. It gave me hope that I could go home soon.

- I then stood back up, returned the shovel to the shed, and went back to his car. The priest drove back to the home he shared with his mother. A few days later, his mother told me that I would be going home and not to worry about ever being hurt by him again. She assured me that her son would never touch me again.

- About a week later the priest drove me home. My parents were glad to see me. They asked if I had fun and I told them I had fun with the priest's mother and we never talked about it again.

Life After the Assaults

- It has been fifty years since the last torturous assault at the priest's home and at the cemetery. Though I remember it all vividly as if it happened yesterday. I will never forget what he did to me. Especially since I still have the scar on my face from the fall on the shovel at the cemetery that night when

I buried my aborted fetus. The engrained scars in my heart, my mind and my spirit are all a daily reminder of this most horrifying experience that should never happen to any child. I was repeatedly raped and beaten by the priest, who also held me captive in his home where the big attack happened.

- I am left with deep-seated wounds I have continued to suffer from, that to this day still haunt me and affect every decision I make as endeavoring to move forward with my current life experience. I strive hard every day to achieve emotional freedom and live a peaceful life.

- Having been brutally assaulted and violated by the priest has further caused me to live a life of deep depression for 50 years. Though having lost the love of my father and all the wonderful opportunities I should have had with him is by far worse than any assault. A price I further paid upon returning home from the priest's summer stay, when I became estranged from my father.

- I have accepted the fact that the priest made poor decisions and caused me pain, but I have never accepted the fact that I lost my father due to the priest's actions and extreme violent behaviors. I was my father's angel and his sweet little ladybug. And he was my hero and my protector. I cannot accept what happened between us as our relationship spiraled to a point of no return.

- Every day as I strive for peace, I try to focus on great things. The good. However, my pain lives in my heart, and as much as I understand the process of healing, it does not happen because I cannot forget the sound of my father's voice and the way he smiled when he saw me running through the field to greet him.

About the Author

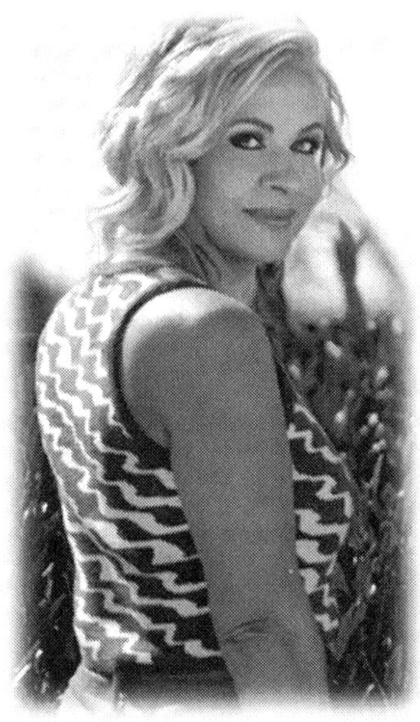

Regina LaFrance has come a long way since leaving her native small village in Southwestern Europe. A place she called home until tragedy struck.

Drawing from her direct experience, her semi-autographical novel, ***Shayla***, is a depiction of the events that happened when she was violently raped as a young girl by a pedophile priest in her village. Her tell-all book further speaks to the deep-seeded wounds and trauma that have followed into her adult life as striving to reinvent herself and find healing.

Shayla is LaFrance's sharing, and ultimate hope, for others who have been molested and suffered from abuse. Passionate in the resolve of this issue, LaFrance has made it her ongoing effort to prevent the unthinkable from happening to more innocent children.

She resides in North Carolina with her husband, Dan, a retired fire lieutenant. Both are transplants from Boston where they met.

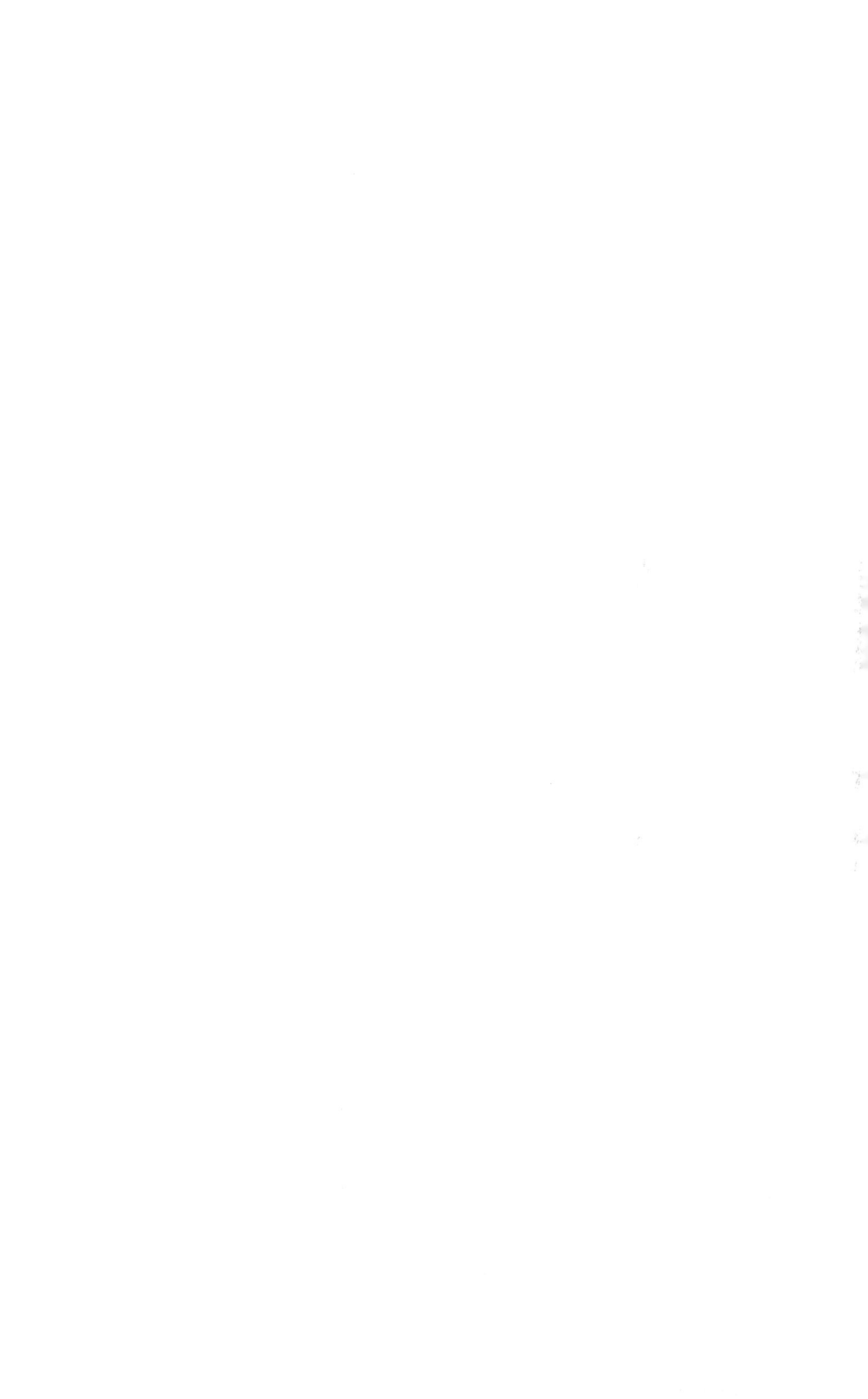

Made in the USA
Columbia, SC
02 June 2024